MILITANT

LIBERTY

IN THIS WORK, NUMEROUS COMPLEX SUBJECTS WILL

BE EXPLORED. NONE ARE INTENDED TO BE

COMPREHENSIVE, ONLY INTRODUCTORY

THE READER IS HIGHLY ENCOURAGED TO

INDEPENDENTLY EXPLORE EACH SUBJECT IN-DEPTH FOR

A WELL-ROUNDED UNDERSTANDING

Table of Contents

THIS WORK IS DEDICATED TO THE NEW
GENERATION OF FREEDOM FIGHTERS.

Chapter 1:

INTRODUCTION TO RELATIONSHIPS

"Teamwork is the ability to work together toward a common vision. The ability to direct individual accomplishments toward organizational objectives. It is the fuel that allows common people to attain uncommon results."

– Andrew Carnegie

By mid-1942, Nazi Germany had conquered much of Europe. Germany had mainland Europe gripped in an iron fist, and the Allies had not yet begun any significant planning of the invasion of Normandy. The Soviet Union, however, had already driven the Germans back from Moscow and had begun focusing its efforts on relieving Stalingrad. As these superpowers collided, the unsuspecting nation of Iran became a pawn in their geopolitical game.

Germany saw Iran as an opportunity to open a new front due to its proximity to the Soviet Union, while the Soviets sought to secure their southern border. Consequently, the Soviet Union began providing support to the fledgling *Tudeh* communist party of Iran as well as arming communist separatists operating in Iran and their northern neighbor, Azerbaijan. Germany had allegedly begun sending arms shipments and encouraging a coup by the nationalist factions of Iran. At the same time, American and English forces began training and organizing Iranian police to beat back the various German and Soviet influences. Fazlollah Zahedi, Army General and Chief of National Police, was a major part of those allied efforts. One of the advisors sent by the United States to assist with the organization and training was Norman Schwarzkopf. Soon after the allies began focusing on Iran, however, Zahedi would be identified as a German collaborator and imprisoned in British Palestine until 1945, but not before he and Schwarzkopf developed close personal ties. After the war ended, Zahedi returned to Iran and was juggled through a number of appointments and positions.

In 1953, Schwarzkopf would also return to Iran and use his connections and friendships, at the behest of the American Central Intelligence Agency, to meet with and convince Mohammad Reza Shah, the monarch of Iran, to use his authority and execute a coup d'état to overthrow the nationalist Prime Minister, Mohammad Mosaddegh. This meeting and the subsequent coups led to a series of disastrous events for Iran and the middle east that would completely transform the region and spawn the dysfunctional nations we know today.

Mohammad Mossadegh, former Iranian PM (pictured with head down)
during his sentencing

Because Schwarzkopf was assigned to Iran in 1942, he was able to meet Zahedi and develop a relationship with him and other Iranians (some being operatives within the highest level of the Iranian government, others being no more than common street thugs), most of whom would go on to participate in the coup with Zahedi. Without the close relationships that he developed, Schwarzkopf may have been unsuccessful in his mission to divide Iran between the Shah (a symbol of Islamic and Persian heritage) and the Prime Minister (a symbol of nationalist destiny and democratization). Had the mission failed, and had western influence in the country waned, Iran may have become a truly functioning state and Iran, who, in the 1940s and 50s, saw

America as a friend, would not be currently funding destabilization efforts in Iraq, Afghanistan, and Syria.

All of this underlines one key point; in ANY political action (regardless of its intention), relationships, and the ability to utilize those relationships in ways that facilitate the completion of objectives, is paramount. Agents such as Schwarzkopf could accomplish nothing if they did not have access to friends and acquaintances that occupy key positions in government, society, or business. Remember this and remember how Schwarzkopf and Zahedi influenced crises and wars that spanned decades simply because they knew how each other, their goals, and how they thought.

By leveraging your relationships with individuals in positions of power or influence, your ability to expand your own influence is increased. Ways you can leverage your relationships can include, but are not limited to:

- Introductions to other *agents of influence* (AOIs)
- Vouching for your effectiveness, discretion, etc. to potential AOIs
- Financing/Loans/Intelligence Gathering
- Alliances/Coalitions/Partnerships
- Logistics/Supply Acquisition
- Safekeeping/Protection
- Propaganda Dissemination

The AOIs that are within your sphere of influence can do all this and more for you, it is just a matter of developing the relationships to where they can be mutually beneficial and worth the risks. AOIs do not necessarily need to be high-level individuals, or people with extreme influence over others. AOIs can be reporters, landlords or real estate agents, and councilmen. The introduction to other, more "valuable" AOIs is often what leads to the more large-scale benefits. For example, CIA agents involved in the Guatemalan Coup of 1954, as well as the intervention in Indonesia in 1957, were able to use the private shipping and air transport capabilities of business tycoons who saw rising communist governments as a threat to their business interests, and thus cooperated with, or even enabled, the CIA to pursue its regime change activities. The CIA and the corporations were brought together by individuals who were coincidentally (or not so coincidentally) connected, and since the proposal was mutually beneficial, the relationship blossomed. By using the commercial transportation donated or lent from valid and established companies, the CIA was able to provide itself a degree of deniability. Without the assistance from their commercial partners, completing their objectives would have been significantly more difficult, if not impossible (efforts in Indonesia ended up largely failing eventually, anyway).

Even Islamic Jihadists and activists in the middle east have shown how important relationships are. In the 1980s, during the Russian invasion of Afghanistan, wealthy Arabs responded to the pleas of the Afghan mujahideen and began donating funds. At one point, Saudi Arabia alone was donating upwards of $20 million every month. Osama Bin Laden travelled from Saudi Arabia to Pakistan in order to use the resources of his construction company to assist the mujahideen. As Afghani envoys began soliciting the Arab and western world for support, others like Bin Laden began donating supplies and funds, eventually leading the Americans to get involved. This part of the relationship yielded arms shipments to the Mujahideen that included anti-aircraft stinger missiles, which helped the mujahideen resist the numerous Soviet air assaults around the country and especially in the Panjshir valley. Such a gift was extremely beneficial since the air power of a conventional force is often untouchable by an unconventional one. This is a prime example of how the AOI system works; you acquire a series of low or mid-level connections, and you develop them. These connections yield their own results over time, and may allow you to, by proxy, acquire new, higher level AOIs. The higher level AOIs yield more resources, provide greater assistance, which may help turn the tide when it is needed most.

Mujahideen posing on downed Soviet MI-8.

Chapter 2:

FINANCING

"If you destroy a Free Market, you create a Black Market."

– **Winston Churchill**

Money is a determining factor in success and comfort for entire nations as well as individuals and families. Money is generally understood to be paper currency, but in reality, money can be anything that we attribute value to and use to trade for other items of value. To this day, we barter for and with goods, scaling from instances as small as farmers markets, all the way up to international trade.

A reliable stream of income is critical for any organization. Corporations have been rendered bankrupt, families have been torn apart, and societies have crumbled due to the simple fact that financial security is a determining factor for success. This rule has been especially true in conflicts. Without money, governments can not raise armies, produce weapons, pay soldiers, transport supplies, or rebuild once the conflict has ended. The pursuit of financing a standing army is straightforward most of the time; divert taxed money to a central military authority (e.g., Department of Defense). However, for unconventional forces, the process can be more complicated and frustrated with obstacles. Due to unconventional forces being at a natural disadvantage to conventional forces, the pursuit of financing has seen much innovation and creativity since, in some cases, Unconventional Groups (Unconventional Groups) cannot simply collect taxes from locals, either due to a lack of authority or shifting territory.

Donations have always been a major source of funding for combatants, especially for unconventional forces. In the previous chapter, we briefly discussed how the Arab world united during the Soviet Invasion of Afghanistan. During this time, donations, or "alms," helped the Mujahideen resist years of Soviet assault. Alms itself is a major facet of the Islamic faith, so they naturally have a system of non-profits and faith organizations that help disseminate these funds to those they deem needy. This system has also been used by Islamic extremists, who have used alms as one major form of funding their Jihad. The Taliban, for example, receives a considerable amount of alms from private donors, but also receives millions of dollars from certain Islamic governments seeking to support either their fundamentalist interpretation of Islam and Sharia law or, formerly, their war against the United States. According to the BBC, the Taliban has an income between $400 million and $1.5 Billion. Much of this comes from a mix of government and private sources from countries such as Pakistan, Saudi Arabia, and Iran. Much of these alms are received thanks to Taliban-affiliated envoys, who are sent to the Islamic world to build connections and tug on the pocketbooks of fundamentalist Imams and businessmen, but also to contact members of those state's intelligence organizations, who funnel state funds to the organization. With these relationships and the mutual goal of Islamic fundamentalism, the envoys are able to return to Afghanistan with additional financial resources that allow the organization to purchase weapons and supplies, bride officials, and expand their abilities to wage war and organize a stable fundamentalist government. The Taliban, as it consolidates power in a modern Afghanistan, will only continue to secure more donations and now, tax or extortion revenue, as shown by the $400 million - $1.5 billion figure.

Another group that received considerable private financial support was the Provisional Irish Republican Army. The PIRA, with the goal of creating a united Ireland, acquired much of its funding from donations. However, they facilitated new means to acquire funding. NORAID, the Irish Northern Aid Committee, was created by Michael Flannery, a veteran of the Irish War for Independence, which raised donations in the United States to send to families of arrested or killed Provos in Ireland. At least some of these funds, while ostensibly being sent only to assist the grieving families, undoubtedly ended up in the hands of actual fighters to facilitate the purchase of arms, explosives, and supplies from abroad. Organizations and groups like NORAID have been used by other groups as well in order to give private donations an air of legitimacy and legality to any observers. Fronts tend to be more common for groups operating in developed nations, or who have international influence.

Another form of aid, which we will call "disorganized aid," comes from the support of the general population when the group in question is popular with the locals. This type of aid can only come from having the support and love of the general population. The list of conflicts and groups that have utilized disorganized aid is too extensive to detail. In every conflict, locals have come out to support these forces by providing tangible goods and services, such as food, water, shelter, protection, forged documentation, intelligence, and many other useful things. The caveat to receiving disorganized aid is that insurgents absolutely must have popular support, otherwise the locals will do the opposite and will likely report their presence or directly participate in operations against them. To achieve popular support, the group must have strong propaganda capabilities. Propaganda will be the focus of a future chapter.

The primary downside to relying on donations is that they can be quite inconsistent. Again, look at the projected earnings of the Taliban and you will see that the income might not only be in constant flux, but that it can also drop at times where it may not be ideal. When Michael Flannery first went to the United States to begin raising money for the anti-treaty IRA, he faced considerable challenges because the United States suffering from the Great Depression, and, despite many Americans having Irish heritage and supporting Irish reunification, they were unable to spare the expense. Economic challenges may be present during times of fundraising and will likely impact the end-result. Another important aspect of fundraising is making sure the correct person(s) has been appointed to the task. Knowing how to use human psychology and negotiation properly is critical for fundraising.

It is important, when setting up NGOs or businesses that have a goal of secretly funding a group, that it is set up as distant as possible from the group itself. This means having all administrative work handled by individuals who have, ideally, no official contact with the group itself. Consider Michael Flannery and NORAID (Northern Ireland Aid committee). Flannery fought in the Irish War for Independence, so he had contacts within the Irish-Republican political sphere, but he emigrated to the United States. The physical distance and the lapse in time between him and his involvement helped provide him and his organization a level of deniability. This deniability is what led him to be able to send all collected aid, which ranged from money to arms and explosives, back to Ireland. Of course, NORAID was eventually investigated, but it was cleared of charges and still operates in a more limited capacity today. Deniability when setting up organizations intent on collecting aid is critical. Without it, authorities will discover the true intention of the organization and will shut it down. This could be catastrophic, especially if income sources are not plentiful or diversified.

Other examples of NGOs being used to funnel aid to groups and organizations are the color revolutions in the early and mid-2000s. These revolutions were mostly peaceful democratic revolutions in former Soviet States, such as Ukraine, Georgia, Kyrgyzstan, and Czechoslovakia. After the fall of the Soviet Union and, with it, the Iron Curtain, it became much easier for western organizations to enter Eastern Europe to organize pro-western groups. Some of the first westerners to enter the region in an official capacity were NGO workers; mostly innocent volunteers who wanted to do good, but covert agents who were planted inside the NGOs by western governments. These NGOs arrived in-country and began meeting with and training local pro-democracy activists and university students in a variety of skills and practices. Some of these were benign, such as media literacy and protest orchestration. Meanwhile, other volunteers trained locals in civil disobedience, resistance, and, in some cases, even encouraged the seizure of government or public buildings. These trainings were coupled with some funding for the revolutions. This deniability exists so long as the NGOs remain distant from the source of their funding or training.

Kyrgyz opposition supporter, Kyrgyz Revolution of 2010

Despite the fluctuating nature of donations from NGOs, private donors, and disorganized aid, they remain a constant source of income for Unconventional Groups for good reason. If the group is fighting a noble fight, defined by cultural, religious, or political practices or motives that can be marketed, it will always be possible to acquire funding of some degree. Caution, discretion, and deniability are words that should be associated with the collection of voluntary aid. Without those attributes, successes will likely be few and far between. It is important to note that NGOs and charities do not get a free pass. Suspicious transactions or potentially fraudulent activity can flag and have the potential to be investigated by state financial authorities.

COMMODITIES & GOODS

Another way groups may secure funding is by operating a commercial wing for their organization. War is, in fact, a business after all. Most successful Unconventional Groups find a way to blur their identity between business, NGO, and militant group. This makes sense, since insurgencies are conducted to support political goals, and are thus involved in other pursuits which insurgency exists only to support or enable. However, in order for the insurgency aspect of the group to be supported, most groups turn to the black-market sale of commodities and goods. These sales are usually considered illegal and are thus interdicted by state authorities or militaries.

A prime example of this would be ISIS's black-market sale of Iraqi and Syrian oil. The sale of the oil provided funding to the group (who's goal was overtly political in nature, as previously stated) despite the sales being considered illegal by most western authorities. However, some states sanctioned the sales and even went as far as purchasing the oil. Turkey, Russia, and Syria were some of the states that purchased the oil. To clarify, if Turkey, ostensibly an American ally as well as a member of NATO, had directly given financial aid to ISIS, it would have likely created a major diplomatic crisis. However, because Turkey indirectly supported ISIS by purchasing their oil there was less of an international outcry. Either way, ISIS got its money.

Examples of commodities and goods that groups have sold include, but are not limited to:

- Oil

- Drugs/Narcotics

- Legal businesses producing legitimate commodities/goods

Groups must be exceedingly careful when pursuing these options, as some of them may be culturally frowned upon. For example, the cultivation of opium poppies is a common practice in places such as Afghanistan, or regions within Southeast Asia. However, opium production in western cultures will be generally frowned upon and will cause friction between the group and the local population; this would be detrimental to the overall political goals. The taboo around Cannabis, on the other hand, has been slowly fading in the western world over the last 2 decades or more. While cultivation is still frowned upon in certain areas, the use of cannabis is generally accepted or tolerated. It is always important to have a very strong understanding of the political, cultural, and social norms in whatever region you intend to operate in. The understanding of such factors, among many others, can be summarily entitled "area study," which we will revisit in Chapter Five's section on Reconnaissance.

Oil consists of entirely different considerations. Oil is not sold directly to consumers. Unconventional Groups are unlikely to completely own oil wells, platforms, or any other production or supply facilities needed. This means that relationships come into play. If the group is able to develop relations with the corporate owners, they may be able to come to a deal based on mutual aid that would yield either a cut of the revenue, or potentially a sanctioned delivery of oil that can be then independently sold by the group. In the case of the ISIS-Turkey oil sales, it was reported that ISIS was not making the deliveries directly to the Turkish government, but to middlemen and shadow buyers who would then smuggle the oil into Turkey and then disappear.

It is important to note that oil will likely not be a primary source of income. ISIS was able to make significant income from its oil sales since it had a semi-conventional force that was able to take and hold territory, as well as the fact that the territory ISIS had taken, particularly the province of Deir Ezzor in Syria, was known to have potent oil production.

Legal businesses are also common. Unconventional Groups will set up new businesses or take over established ones, and then use the clean money coming from them to fund their activities. Some traditional and common examples of this include car dealerships, taxi companies, and garbage companies, but this can be implemented with just about any legally operating business. An amount of the revenue will be siphoned off in small amounts so as to not attract attention and will be delivered to the group. Again, caution, discretion, and deniability are key. The business should have no clear connections to the organization, and it should operate as a normal business, providing only a small amount of the revenue every so often. This is why the traditional examples (taxis, car dealerships, etc.) are chosen, because there can be many of them and it is very common to have money pass through the business and into other money streams or assets, thus making the link between the business and the organization difficult to track. Obscuring the connection altogether is preferred but having the revenue pass through multiple hands before reaching the organization is good.

Groups may also secure funding by providing services to the local population. This section is limited and is only included to provide a well-rounded appreciation for how groups have been financed in the past. Some of these practices have been extremely detrimental to those implementing them and can be directly tied to the failure of certain groups to achieve their strategic goals.

Some of these services include, but are not limited to:

- Counterfeiting
- Loan Sharking
- Protection Rackets
- Smuggling

Some, if not all, of these examples can be extremely lucrative and predatory at the same time. From a pragmatic point of view, the ends may justify the means, but when the situation involves an insurgency, or any unconventional force opposing an established power, moral superiority is always key. When a group begins shaking down locals for every penny they have, they soon are seen not as freedom fighters, but as common thugs.

This was the case with the Provisional IRA. The Provos began running rackets of all kinds. They smuggled weapons into residential areas and peddled drugs to children and teens. Early on,

IRA leadership recognized that drugs had no place in their communities and punished offenders, but, eventually, they embraced the revenue. These practices, along with the IRAs use of civilian casualties to coerce British cooperation, led them to be disliked and hated by many in Northern Ireland. Without the support of the people (the importance of which will be explored in Chapter 4), the Provos could not possibly hope to drive the British from Northern Ireland. The IRA continued to fragment into splinter groups. Now, a shell of it exists, and the members who did not join Sinn Fein (the political party representing Irish-Republican interests), are now little more than drug dealers and criminals, fighting not to reunify Ireland, but for opportunity; a leg up on their fellow Irishman.

A similar situation also occurred during the American Revolution, especially during times of hardship. Patriots and Continentals would sometimes raid homesteads for food and supplies after major battles and during the winter stay at Valley Forge. This, of course, caused many people to hate the American cause. While the result was not disastrous for them, it did create unnecessary tension with the moderates, turning them into loyalists. Many of those people hated the idea of America so much by the end of the war that they fled to Britain, British Canada, and even India. The impression that fighters give to the average person directly ties into how the entire group is perceived, which determines the level of support the group will enjoy. Every fighter is a diplomat and must carry themselves as such.

With care, some services could be lucrative and morally sound. However, a group must be cautious, as the pursuit of money is always capable of corrupting the goal. If the strategic goal of political change is lost in the pursuit of money or petty influence, then the intention will be picked up by the populace and the group will share the same fate as the Provisional IRA.

Unconventional groups may also get their funding from legitimate or semi-legitimate businesses. Typically, these businesses are ones that do not require any significant professional licensing or startup costs. They may also be businesses where cash transactions occur regularly and where income may fluctuate, such as taxi companies, night clubs, or bars. Additionally, any influx or efflux of funds (*especially* electronic fund transfers) that are inconsistent with normal business operations or are otherwise unexplainable may be flagged by Anti-money Laundering (AML) teams at financial institutions or financial crime units within law enforcement, for investigation. Flagging is also more likely if there are direct ties between the business and any militant or criminal activity. In cases of the successful utilization of legitimate businesses, the siphoning of funds to unconventional groups tends to be few and far between or may consist of smaller deposits and withdrawals. The key is to diversify and have access to several legitimate businesses, which will make up for the small withdrawals that will come from each of them.

Other sources may include self-funding, that is, using one's own businesses or financial sources to support a group. An example that has been mentioned before is Osama Bin Laden using his fortune gained from his family's construction company, the Saudi Binladin Group, to funnel arms and money to the Mujahideen in Afghanistan via the Hindu Kush Mountains and Pakistan. Bin Laden also co-founded *Maktab al-Khidamat,* or the Afghan Services Bureau, to assist in the funneling of aid as well as the coordination with Pakistan's Inter-Services Intelligence (ISI) agency and the Saudi Arabian General Intelligence Presidency (GIP). This group assisted Arabs and Muslims going to Pakistan with travel and training, it legally paid or bribed Pakistani authorities, and it established militant training camps in the hinterlands of western Pakistan and Eastern Afghanistan.

Maktab al-Khidamat established offices and liaisons within American refugee camps along the east coast, as well as within international aid groups, NGOs, and charities to further their goals. While the legality of *Maktab al-Khidamat* and the Saudi Binladen Group's end goal of funneling aid, arms, and fighters to Afghanistan may be debatable, their existence itself was not. Bin Laden and others would use these legal enterprises and the funds from them to fund their semi-legal (and eventually openly illegal) activities. Of course, the illegal connections were eventually known, and were shut down, disintegrated, or heavily monitored and today it is generally accepted that the Saudi Binladen Group is entirely legitimate in its activities.

At the end of the day, the transfer of funds from legitimate, semi-legitimate, and illegal activities to the unconventional group should be done as surreptitiously as possible. Traditional financial institutions and networks have become extensively monitored by both law enforcement and financial institutions themselves. If funds are discovered to be from or for illegal, semi-legal, or sanctioned groups or activities, then the funds will be confiscated and involved parties could face investigation or arrest, causing further complications for the unconventional group. This is where decentralized currencies come into play.

Cryptocurrency is a fully digital decentralized currency that is based on blockchain technology and secured by cryptography. A blockchain is a digital database that records and stores information, usually transaction data (deposits, withdrawals, transfers). Each block in the blockchain is filled with data, and when it reaches capacity, it is locked and timestamped, preventing alteration or fabrication. The blockchain is just a chronologically recorded series of transactions. Additionally, the data in the blockchain is not held at a single location but is shared among thousands and thousands of inter-connected computers, spread out across the globe. This decentralized nature prevents the currency from being reliant on a single point of failure, such as a bank or a server. While it is not impossible, the cost and energy required to disrupt or steal most cryptocurrencies would be unachievable without alerting currency holders, who would just create a new fork in the blockchain that has not been altered, returning any bad actor to square one, having wasted an immense amount of time and resources.

Because the blockchain stores the transaction history securely, it removes the need for a third party (such as a private or central bank) to step in and manage the transactions. By removing the need for the third party, it also removes their authority over the currency. Most modern currencies are fiat currencies, meaning that they are not backed by any commodity, like gold or silver. Fiat currencies only have value because the parties that use it agree that it has a predetermined value (we all agree that a $1 bill is worth exactly $1, not more or less). However, through manipulation, ineptitude, and predatory actions, banks and governments can destabilize and devalue the currency, reducing the buying power and directly harming citizen users. An example of such predation and ineptitude would be the Global Financial Crisis of 2008.

Alternative to fiat currency, cryptocurrency value is based on its blockchain and supply and demand of the currency. Some cryptocurrencies, such as Ethereum, have an unlimited supply, similar to fiat currencies in that paper currency can be infinitely printed by a central authority. Others, like Bitcoin, have a finite supply that directly influences its value. The more popular the currency, the more its value, and, correspondingly, its buying power. With Bitcoin, value cannot be manipulated by a single actor, such as a government. Instead, it is a collective market that determines value. As of 2021, cryptocurrencies had an aggregate value of $2.1 trillion, a value that exceeds the nominal GDP of most developed nations. While cryptocurrencies are not accepted as tender everywhere, they are very quickly becoming accepted, and can be exchanged for fiat currencies.

Cryptocurrencies can be acquired through simply exchanging fiat currencies for cryptocurrency at rate, like any other currency exchange, or they can be mined. Mining allows new units of currency to enter circulation. Mining also plays a critical role in providing legitimacy to cryptocurrency transactions. Mining can be extremely difficult and costly, as it requires powerful machines and an immense amount of power to solve complex mathematical problems. These problems can be solved by using advanced Graphics Processing Units (GPUs). The miner needs to solve the equations before other miners and needs to validate existing blocks in the blockchain in order to receive payment in the currency. This competition is called *Proof of Work*. Alternatively, *Proof of Stake* still requires the transactions to be validated, but instead, the validators are randomized and are then paid for their contributions.

Utilizing cryptocurrency may allow unconventional groups to continue to access the free market and finance their groups and activities. It prevents central authorities from controlling or manipulating their access to funding or a free market, as well as helping the general public achieve the same thing

Chapter 3:

LOGISTICS & SUSTAINMENT

"Clearly, logistics is the hard part of fighting a war."
- Lt. Gen. E. T. Cook

In 1812, Napoleon Bonaparte invaded Russia. Up until this point, he had conquered much of Europe and defeated the great Empires of the west. His decisions singlehandedly set a new course for European history. However, he made significant miscalculations when planning the invasion. His army consisted of 500,000 men, backed by thousands upon thousands of support personnel, horses, and wagons. When he entered Russian territory, the Russians burned everything and retreated. Russian peasants attacked French supply wagons from a distance and armed partisans killed anyone who wandered too far from the line. Eventually, outside of Moscow, the Russians faced the French. The Battle of Borodino was the bloodiest recorded battle in history up until that moment, with upwards of 70,000 men killed in a single day. After this, the Russian army retreated and the French occupied Moscow. But the French did not enjoy victory for long, as the infamous Russian winter began to set in.

Napoleon had stretched his long, cumbersome army dangerously thin while pursuing the Russians. And now, as the Russians retreated once again, parts of Moscow were set ablaze so the French could not have it. Russian peasants killed any French foragers who ambled into the wrong apartment or village searching for bread. Suddenly, Napoleon had almost nothing due to a variety of factors; the distance between himself and friendly territory, the scorched-earth policy the Russians implemented, and the vast needs of his army. After five weeks, he abandoned the city and his army marched miles in freezing temperatures, with snow up to men's thighs in some cases. Tens of thousands of men would freeze or starve to death. There were no medical supplies remaining, so anyone seriously wounded at Borodino also had slim chances of survival.

Napoleon, in his race to swiftly defeat the Russians, seemed to have forgotten everything he had ever learned about supplying his forces.

When Napoleon set out for Russia, he had close to half a million men. He returned to France with 100,000.

In any conflict, the ability to keep your forces supplied is critical. Without a well-thought-out logistics pipeline, the likelihood of success is extremely poor. In this chapter, we will explore how groups, primarily unconventional in nature, might establish efficient logistics pipelines to facilitate their strategic and tactical goals.

BLACK MARKETS

In a truly free society, a person should be able to engage in voluntary interactions between other people. However, this is not the reality, unfortunately. Government restrictions and social taboos prevent us from achieving a truly free society. Because of this, we have formed black markets.

In essence, a black market is simply the supply and demand of goods or services that are either considered illegal by state authorities or are highly regulated, restricting the general public's ability to legally acquire those goods. Additionally, black markets are not inherently bad or morally wrong. Of course, there are illegal markets for drugs, weapons, and even people, but there are also "illegal" markets that traffic in harmless commodities, like cheaper medications or treatment from other industrialized nations, baby formula, commodities from sanctioned or embargoed states, and even fake social media accounts. When your neighbor fixes your sink for a small fee without a license, you are participating in the black market. Whenever the Government decides to outlaw an item or service that they cannot tax, license, or otherwise exploit, a black market emerges. For the sake of this chapter, we will focus on how groups utilize black markets, and not the morality or legality thereof.

Weapons have formed the base of black markets for thousands of years. Where social hierarchies exist, those in power have tried to limit the general population from owning weapons, sometimes for valid public safety concerns (which does not absolve criminal behavior, such as the disarmament of a free and innocent people), but predominantly for reasons of power consolidation. Because of this, black markets develop to funnel weapons to criminal and political groups. In this section, we will focus on the cartels of Latin America, since they operate simultaneously as business entities as well as insurrectionary groups.

Occasionally, cartels would get supplies from foreign states. The Sinaloa Cartel received such support from the CIA and the ATF in order to weaken other cartels who were much less organized and significantly more violent, but such support tends to be the exception, not the rule. Historically, these groups get their weapons from violent clashes with government, military, or police forces, as well as by using the relationships the groups have developed with AOIs. If a cartel has a working relationship with a local or regional security official, that relationship could yield a relatively steady flow of supplies. Or they may simply attack a poorly defended armory or convoy and abscond with the supplies within.

Mexican soldiers patrol in El Limoncito, Mexico after a battle for territory between local gangs, the Sinaloa cartel, and government forces

Additionally, cartels get many of their firearms from international trade with other groups. In some cases, cartels will send operatives abroad (similarly to how the Afghan mujahideen did) in order to acquire aid and develop relationships. This practice is mainly used in the U.S., where operatives will shop around in the South-Western U.S. and legally purchase firearms to be smuggled back into Mexico. Through corrupt officials in central America, they receive surplus supplies brought in for the drug war, including weapons such as mortars, grenade launchers, heavy machine guns, explosives, and even anti-tank weapons. The Jalisco New Generation Cartel is noted as having used RPGs, likely brought in from overseas connections, to bring down Mexican military and police helicopters. Much of the military-grade weaponry was acquired from Mexican Army deserters who fled with supplies. Using relationships with established AOIs and direct confrontation with security forces, cartels are able to maintain a steady supply of a wide-ranging arsenal in a country that maintains strict anti-gun laws.

Outside of Mexico and the U.S., Cartels have operations in Asian and European markets. By exporting what they offer (drugs, mainly, but also human trafficking and money laundering services), they can extend their reach to available markets where firearms may be illegal but are readily available. *Armament Research Services*, an intelligence consulting firm, has identified weapons in Mexico with origins in Europe. In former Warsaw Pact countries (especially Moldova and Bulgaria, but also throughout the region), weapon dumps are abundant and are often monitored poorly by local officials who may be susceptible to subornation. As of 2020, Mexico's Secretariat of National Defense estimates that one third of all weapons smuggled into Mexico arrived from Europe. The fact that these countries are rife with corruption is also important to note, as the corrupt nature of state officials is what enables the arrangement.

For groups operating outside of the law, engaging with the black market is often a necessity for survival. The black market, of course, receives plenty of attention from authorities seeking to dismantle it. Caution, of course, should be taken. If authorities identify the market and who engages in it, the loss of access to whatever the market supplied could be potentially devastating.

Another important aspect of logistics is field procurement. Field procurement, at its core, is simply the collection of resources within an operating area instead of being encumbered by a lengthy supply chain. As discussed in the previous section, Mexican cartels often acquired their arsenal from field procurement after fighting security forces and seizing what they could in the aftermath of the fight. In fact, field procurement has been used by every unconventional force to some degree. The Vietcong collected weapons from US and ARVN forces. The Mujahideen collected AK47s and RPGs from Soviet convoys and slain soldiers. The Sicarii picked up knives and swords off of dead romans.

Even Sun Tzu talked about the importance of field procurement.

"Hence a wise general makes a point of foraging on the enemy. One cartload of the enemy's provisions is equivalent to twenty of one's own, and likewise a single picul of his provender is equivalent to twenty from one's own store."

Field procurement is not limited to weapons. It includes any supplies that might be useful, including food, shelter, transportation, and just about anything else that can be collected from the enemy or nature, or is willingly given by locals. From a purely practical standpoint, groups should be careful about field procurement, in that they either only take from hostile forces (and NOT from locals) or, if the supplies needed are controlled by locals, only take what is freely given or can be returned or repaid. Mao Zedong and his army won the support of the Chinese peasantry by respecting them and their possessions. In Mao's teachings to his army, he made it a point to establish rules such as "Return all borrowed articles" and "No confiscation of people's property." The relationship between Mao's Red Army and the peasant class of China became a symbiotic one. Without the support of the Peasants, the Army would have lost its primary source of recruitment but also its source of food. Of course, these rules and expectations were disregarded when Mao consolidated his power and began confiscating land and weapons from those he saw as political opponents, including many of the peasants who had helped him during the long march.

Sun Tzu, when speaking on logistics, focused primarily on food, and feeding his forces. Armies in ancient China were massive, and scavenged supplies on a large scale, often from entire regions, and not simply from towns or individual fields, likely implementing taxes or quotas for producers to meet after the army gained control of the town or region. For most unconventional groups, field procurement is done on a significantly smaller scale, especially in the context of food. In most western societies, food is plentiful and is not difficult to find. In the U.S., 30-40 percent of all food produced (roughly 133 billion pounds) is wasted, being thrown away due to excess or poor appearance. Excess food can be found in restaurant and market dumpsters, often packaged somewhat neatly and (mostly) free from exposure.

Additionally, the U.S. is abundant in wild game. Hunting and trapping are common activities and many people begin hunting at a young age. Hunted game can become a main source of food for any group operating out the wilderness. This is less effective for large groups, due to the mass of energy needed, but is sufficient for smaller groups operating independently over a large area.

Water especially is critical to any force, but especially to unconventional forces trekking long distances. Individuals should aim to have 4-6 liters in their kit, or roughly one liter per two hours of patrolling (this amount, of course, depends on climate, activity, water availability, etc.). Additionally, everyone should have the knowledge and means to safely collect, filter, and purify drinking water. Water purification tablets can also be employed if available. Untreated water may contain disease-causing bacteria, protozoa, viruses, as well as chemical pollutants, metals, or excreta. The implications of consuming impure water will be explored in a later section.

In contested environments, individuals should be cautious while collecting water. They should access the water source from an unlikely direction and be quick with their collection. Individuals should also make sure that they are thoroughly cleaning any drinking or cooking equipment that has been in contact with impure water, as those surfaces may have traces of bacteria or pollutants.

Every country has facilities that produce firearms, ammunition, and ordnance. Throughout Europe and the United States, these facilities are often operated by civilian-run defense contractors. The supplies are then transported via road or rail to other, often more secure locations for storage. The most vulnerable points in this chain are during transport.

Defense companies often assist governments and militaries in their counterinsurgent activities. These companies produce goods from factories and warehouses that have physical locations, often in unsecure sites in rural or peri-urban areas. Additionally, the goods, tools, weapons, and equipment that are produced are often transported by civilian-run companies. Such companies use all modes of transport; road, rail, air, and ship. This section has been left intentionally vague.

Many unconventional groups eventually lose access to logistics pipelines they may have had when they first began operating. When this happens, it is paramount that adaptability is prioritized so other pipelines can be accessed and utilized. When it becomes impossible to access alternate sources, the responsibility of producing the supplies falls on the end user. A surprising number of tools and equipment used on 20th and 21st century battlefields can be reproduced or even improved upon with commercially available components.

One example that is very recent is the rise and fall of the Islamic State. Throughout their violent crusade in Iraq and Syria, professional engineers and chemists with scholarly backgrounds had joined their ranks. As ISIS expanded its territory and captured supplies from the Iraqi army began to run dry, it created factories that mass produced increasingly lethal weapons. Miniature explosives disguised as rocks (similar in effect to Viet Cong cartridge traps), home-made mortar tubes and mortar shells, grenades and mortars specially engineered to be deployed from drones, and RPG warheads altered to include components such as mustard agents and caustic soda were all produced. They managed to do this by repurposing common metal and melting it down to fit inside homemade molds. They would also use commonly found 119.2mm water pipes as mortar tubes, and their engineering could be extremely precise, down to a 10th of a millimeter. ISIS was even able to mass-produce a proprietary plastic explosive, mostly made from ammonium nitrate and aluminum paste, to be used in RPGs, mortar shells, and IEDs. From an engineering perspective, ISIS was brilliant and was exponentially more advanced than most insurgencies. This is in part due to their strategic goal of establishing an official state, or caliphate, and not simply taking over an already established state like the Taliban. They also took advantage of supplies and infrastructure that were already available.

The IRA also used its engineering know-how to develop artillery that would be used to attack British positions in Ireland, as well as in England. Numerous models of these cannons, known as Barrack Busters, have been developed and used by other unconventional groups abroad, including the Free Syrian Army. Early Barrack Busters were poorly made, especially the mortar tube itself. However, the shell itself had a devastating impact. Itself just a propane tank, the shell would be loaded with the explosives that the IRA had on hand, usually Semtex, and was simply lobbed into British barracks, hence the name. While this mortar did not exactly turn the tide for the IRA, it did force the British to pull many of their bases and checkpoints away from the border between the Republic of Ireland and Northern Ireland. It also forced British forces to spend time and resources to reinforce checkpoints and barracks. It had a considerable psychological impact on British forces.

Unconventional Groups could also consider employing technology that has since become out-of-date, such as the Livens projector. Like the Barrack Buster, the Livens projector was just a metal tube that delivered a simple payload. Dug into the earth at a 45° angle, it launched a metal tank filled with chemical weapons or high explosives in large waves due to its general inaccuracy. The Livens projector was cheap and simple, and modern groups could learn from it and, potentially, improve the design to be used alongside modern tools.

The DIY approach to developing weapons has evolved from simply repurposing scrap into weaponry into a new age of engineering and ingenuity. Today, firearms, tools, and even ammunition components can be made in the average garage or basement by using 3D printing. There is a misconception that 3D printed firearms are unreliable, but this is not true. Many 3D firearm models, when printed and designed correctly, can successfully run through thousands of rounds before failure. And considering the capability to produce these units cheaply and quickly, that more than compensates for their being less durable than their steel and polymer counterparts. In nations and states where firearm possession is heavily restricted, the use of 3D printing and downloads of blueprints have seen an incredible surge. This is especially true in Europe, Canada, Oceania, and South America. 3D printing firearms allows for the creation of a completely decentralized supply pipeline of firearms, and potentially even ammunition components. This is especially important due to the increased interest in controlling the importation and exportation of firearms and ammunition from certain places (such as the 2021 Russian ammunition ban) and the renewed push for gun control in 2022. In recent years, increased efforts in research & development have led to innovations in the production of suppressors, sears, braces and stocks, and smaller, more concealable weapons as well as full length rifles.

It would be irresponsible to not mention the fluctuation of logistical availability. Famine and government/militant control of resources has long been a characteristic of war-torn states. This system of centralized forces having control of most (if not all) logistics pipelines in a civil conflict would be reflected in any western country, should one destabilize. Governments will always seize control of food, weapons, ammunition, and every other resource that could be useful for either side. This is especially true in cities, where food is often guarded and rationed by security forces, and where supply chains may be tightly monitored. Therefore, it is imperative that successful Unconventional Groups establish, identify, or prepare its own logistical pipelines.

With the right knowledge, and access to readily available supplies, it is possible to create force multipliers that will give insurgencies significant advantages. It is simply a matter of having access to the right people, such as engineers, who can draw up accurate and safe plans, develop prototypes, and create final products than can be used in the field.

Electronic waste, or E-waste, is any technology that is thrown away or scrapped because the technology has been broken or has seemingly lost its usefulness. In 2009, there were 2.37 million tons of E-waste, 75% of which (1.7 million tons) was not recycled and ended up sitting unused in American landfills. Since then that number has skyrocketed, and the technology that NASA engineers could have used in the 1950s is now littering the ground across the U.S. In each of those electronics that are seemingly worthless, there are millions of semiconductors, visual displays, power supplies, motherboards, timing circuits, motors, fans, sensors, antennas, and hundreds of millions (or perhaps billions) of miles of copper wiring. The inventive guerrilla might access one of the many landfills, recycling centers, or garbage plants and find creative uses for the various pieces of technology that the average person has seen no use in.

Diving for E-waste is not abnormal. Guerrillas have done it before, and it is often one of their standard practices. The Taliban and Al-Qaeda, for example, became known for their use of Improvised Explosive Devices (IEDs), oftentimes using scavenged soviet era artillery shells, fireworks, and wiring.

Guerrilla forces rarely get their way, and this is especially true when it comes to gear and weaponry. Guerrilla groups need to be able to adapt to what is common or readily available, in terms of gear & equipment, arms, and ammunition. Note how insurgent groups throughout central and east Asia are synonymous with the Kalashnikov platform. This is, of course, due to their proximity to the former Soviet Union and the People's Republic of China, and the proliferation of the platform throughout their spheres of influence. The case is the same for the Taliban, who utilized arms and explosives left over from the Soviet-Afghan war. Following the war, various groups in Afghanistan (including the Taliban and the Northern Alliance) were able to continue getting AKs, explosives, RPGs, and other weapons from its northern neighbors and

Pakistan. These groups simply did not have access to the European or American markets and made do with the market they were in.

While the Taliban was fighting with Soviet hand-me-down weapons, the Provisional IRA was fighting the British Empire with a more diverse and local arsenal. Due to their location, the IRA was able to tap into the European arms market. Their arsenal included firearms from Belgium, Sweden, Germany, the United Kingdom, the United States, Czechoslovakia, and various Soviet States along the Baltic Sea. These nations were in close proximity to Ireland and the IRA was able to develop trade and smuggling networks that allowed them to acquire the weapons. Additionally, and somewhat uniquely, the IRA was able to diplomatically secure several arms shipments from Libyan leader Muammar Gaddafi, including Soviet DShK heavy machine guns, AKs (of course), RPG-7s, explosives, and various other Soviet-made weapons and ammunition. They also received arms from the United States (often smuggling via ocean liners or fishing trawlers), where firearm ownership was much less restrictive than in Europe

IRA arms shipments were always at risk of being captured, and such was the case with the Libyan ship *Eksund*. This required the IRA to have other means of acquiring arms, which they did, via the European continent and transatlantic connections in America.

Adaptability is critical for these groups to succeed. Becoming too reliant on one type of weapon, or one source for supplies, can result in catastrophe for the group. Leadership should be constantly reviewing active pipelines and seeking contingency pipelines.

Chapter 4:

PROPAGANDA

"This is the secret of propaganda: To totally saturate the person, whom the propaganda wants to lay hold of, with the ideas of the propaganda, without him even noticing that he is being saturated."

- Paul Watzlawick

The concept of "Hearts and Minds" is not new, but the phrase itself was popularized in Vietnam, and has been used since in Afghanistan and Iraq. In fact, every effective insurgency and counterinsurgency implement some kind of "Hearts and Minds" campaign. It has always been necessary for revolutionary groups and governments alike to have and maintain the support of the general population. The general population is the easiest group to manipulate (due to the herd nature of human beings, especially in collectivist societies) and it is why propaganda is so common and effective. It is simply a matter of understanding the audience, as well as their psychology. With this information, it is possible to tailor messaging to the audience that can manipulate emotions, alter support, and even compel action. In this chapter, we will explore some of the ways propaganda is used, disseminated, and how it can impact people.

At its core, propaganda is simply a form of communication whose intent is to change the way a person or group thinks. The term is neither positive nor negative, as many of us have been led to believe. It is used during wartime to drum up support and to weaken and dehumanize enemies, but it also used by advertisers in peacetime, who seek to activate your base emotions and drives to encourage you to buy their product. Propagandists want to alter your perception of information and events in an attempt to persuade you to their side, usually with the intent of doing so without you even knowing that there were outside pressures influencing the decision. Individuals are targeted, of course, but the grand goal is to influence massive blocs of people and then mobilize them towards a goal. That is the ultimate purpose of propaganda, and it can be summarized as "strength in numbers."

The goal with targeting individuals or groups within the enemy force is to convert them to your cause or demoralize them. Ideally, they will either defect or they will remain to subvert the enemy. Historically, normal methods would be used to reach enemy forces (radio broadcasts, leaflets, etc.) that targeted their morale, often following a defeat. These efforts would also use rumors and hearsay (often fabricated) to further confuse and disorient the enemy following a conflict or event. Either way, converting the enemy force adds to the sum of your own strength and weakens the enemy at the same time.

In any successful venture, whether it is rooted in political discourse, military conflict, or everyday capitalism, it is critical to success that you be able to reach out to the target audience and appeal to them, either directly (consciously) through messaging, or indirectly (unconsciously) through symbolism. If you are unable to do this, it can be very difficult to elicit any kind of response from the target audience, even if they are naturally inclined to support your message. If the propaganda a group disseminates is not tailored to the audience and does not serve the expressed goal of weakening the enemy or altering the opinions of the general public, it is bound to be ineffective and a waste of resources.

Most advancements in communication have all occurred within the last 300 years or so. With the advent of the printing press, literacy becoming the standard, and with new forms of media emerging just decades and now mere years apart, businessmen and generals alike have recognized how important it is to have a presence in all forms of media, but have scrambled to adapt to such rapid developments. Along with the study of communication itself, there has also been abundant study of psychology and how the human mind reacts to various forms of stimuli.

For example, if an individual believes in patriotism, it would be possible to target propaganda to them that could elicit aggression, pride, or even strengthen preconceived biases towards other groups. This specific example could work with several different techniques of propaganda, including a technique known as flag-waving. Even more specifically, examples of flag-waving can be seen during conflicts (especially conflicts involving Americans) following an attack of the homeland or an attack on a close ally. Following 9/11 and the invasions of Iraq and Afghanistan, a wave of hyper-American music, art, and rhetoric came to the forefront of American life, and those who opposed the wars were seen as anti-American, and in some cases were even called traitors. During the first few years, especially during the period where the shock of 9/11 was still wearing off, the hyper-American sentiment could be described almost as euphoric. Again, we can see this attitude during and immediately after World War II, especially during the occupation and de-Nazification of Germany, where the messaging began to shift from attacking Nazis to attacking communists.

The intention during these times was to rouse public opinion at home and abroad by declaring what a just and glorious cause the Americans were embarking on. By doing so, propagandists were able to increase domestic morale while also targeting the enemy of the propaganda. In this case, it was the soviets. Western propaganda (and, of course, the poor living conditions and tyranny in the Soviet Union) became so strong that the Soviets and East Germans had to erect the Berlin Wall just to stop hemorrhaging their population. The propaganda used at the time targeted communism itself, but especially the communist leadership, regularly pointing out the unfair treatment east Germans experienced and also the failures of the communist leadership. Another technique was to point out how prosperous and safe the west was. This was effective because

Eastern Europe was ravaged by the war and was still struggling to recuperate. Even for those who were unable to escape the Soviet Union, western propaganda still reached inside and lit fires in the hearts of young people. It can be argued that these instances of constant propaganda are what led Soviet leadership to gradually weaken, allowing holes to open up in the Iron Curtain. Once those holes were opened, Western influences began to flood In, and everything from Levi jeans (which were seen as a symbol of democracy and freedom) to oil companies were embraced. Despite the Cold War being one of the tensest periods in human history, the situation was not defused by global war or covert regime change, but by a constant, structured stream of propaganda and information warfare aimed at the people within communist states. The Soviets did the same thing, though through less direct means. Today, despite the U.S. having seemingly won the Cold War, communism and socialism are common in cities and especially on college campuses. Though the soviets are long gone, they can rest easily in their graves knowing that many of Americas scholars still proliferate their ideas.

Aside from the flag-waving and gaslighting that was common in the Cold War (and is, to an extent, still common today) there are dozens of other techniques that are used in propaganda. In this section, we will cover only a few for the sake of being concise.

- _Association_: This technique is used to project qualities onto associates of a person, group, or organization so that the audience views the associate and the person, group, or organization as being one-and-the-same. These qualities can be positive or negative. It may also be known as "guilty by association" or "virtuous by association."
- _Virtue Signaling_: This technique is used by attaching positive attributes to an argument, thereby making it naturally good and worthy of support, and then using that argument, regardless of whether or not it is valid. This is done with the intent to make the presenter seem moral or virtuous, without necessarily being so.
- _Straw Man_: A straw man is an attempt to intentionally misinterpret the oppositions statements or positions in order to more easily attack an argument or idea that is not being argued or supported. This technique may encourage the opposition to stoop-down and correct the straw man, which could make them look weak and pliable.

- *Repetition*: This technique is used by repeating a statement, claim, or image in an attempt to make it seem like a common truth, or to simply associate the statement, claim, or imagery with something or someone, positive or negative. This tactic is used in almost every propaganda campaign and is especially common within the corporate media.
- *Latitudes of Acceptance*: This technique is all about making the official stances of a person or group look more moderate or acceptable by having another group espouse even more radical messaging.
- *Fear, Uncertainty, and Doubt*: This technique uses negative emotions to help control and manipulate perceptions and opinions. Negative emotions are among the strongest and can be unpredictable once they are tapped into. Fear, Uncertainty, and Doubt were very common during cold war propaganda campaigns because it encourages unrest and instability, and the proliferation of nuclear weapons made this technique an easy choice.
- *Divide and Conquer*: This technique is used to divide a strong opposition and encourage fragmentation. This can be done by creating rumors, sewing doubt, and using blackmail or smears to target important persons within the opposition. The goal is to target individuals at first to fracture trust, like the cracking of a pane of glass. Gradually, as trust among the group is eroded, the cracks will spread until the glass shatters. As unity disintegrates, the once strong opposition becomes easier to conquer.

These are only a few examples out of many. There are people who spend their entire lives dedicated to understanding propaganda. If any group intends to be successful in its pursuits, whether it is in pursuit of Liberty or otherwise, it needs elements within it who are completely dedicated to understanding and effectively implementing propaganda against its opposition.

There are different delivery platforms that propaganda can be disseminated through. Each has its strengths and weaknesses, and not all of them may be ideal for any given situation. To understand the strengths and weaknesses of delivery platforms, we will look at a few and discuss examples of each.

1. Word of Mouth

Word of Mouth is the oldest delivery platform, and historically among the most effective. Once rumors or ideas begin, they tend to take on a life of their own. Word of Mouth is also the least truthful. As dissemination occurs, the original meaning or intent of the message is often distorted. This is apparent in the children's game 'Telephone', where a simple message is passed along but it gradually becomes more and more ridiculous as people repeat it. If such a phenomenon can occur within the boundaries of a children's game, imagine how much more complicated propaganda dissemination is, and how much more disastrous the implications of a failed campaign could be. However, despite this drawback, Word of Mouth remains the cheapest and most accessible form of delivery. It also requires, of course, propagandists to openly share their message, which could be dangerous.

2. Print Media

Print media can include newspapers, leaflets, and posters, all of which are extremely common methods of delivery. In 18th century New England, most printing presses belonged to patriots. This meant that most newspapers were churning out anti-British media. Whenever an event happened, such as the Boston Massacre or any of the various powder alarms, it was expected that newspapers from Boston to Philadelphia would lay into the British. This system was a decentralized propaganda machine, and it allowed important patriots such as

Samuel Adams and Benjamin Franklin to disseminate articles, op-eds, and letters across the colonies at great speed, faster than the British could possibly quash any rumors or claims.

Another great example of print media are airborne leaflets. Forces have been using hydrogen balloons, airplanes, and artillery cannisters to send leaflets into enemy territory since at least the 19th century. During World War 1, similar tactics were used, but the advent of the airplane helped speed these efforts up. It was now possibly to directly deliver leaflets into enemy trenches. These leaflets often encouraged desertion and insubordination. They also focused on things like rapidly rising death counts and how soldiers were far away from their families. In Vietnam, leaflets (and radio, which is discussed next), encouraged black soldiers to desert, on account of the civil rights movement and the mistreatment of black people in the U.S. These were intended to weaken the opposition forces through morale loss and attrition.

These methods are still viable on a modern battlefield. In fact, they have been used extensively in Korea, Vietnam, Iraq, Afghanistan, and even Syria. Print media is still useful in the 21st century.

3. Radio

Following the 1930s, ownership of radios began to skyrocket across the world. As this rise in radio ownership happened, companies and governments began to see them as opportunities. As the United States endured and recovered from the Great Depression, Americans from all over tuned in to hear advertisements and political speeches. Franklin Delano Roosevelt took advantage of radio to begin his Fireside Chats, a series of addresses used to talk about pressing national issues. These addresses contributed to FDRs popularity at the time. The Fireside Chats were a form of propaganda, as FDR used his excellent communication skills to convince Americans that his policies, programs, and actions were worthy of being implemented or were already working. It also added a level of apparent transparency that many Americans felt to be refreshing.

Of course, radio broadcasts became even more common with the onset of World War II and especially the Cold War. Broadcasts from US and European forces were common during wartime. In World War II, from the allied side, domestic broadcasts encouraged perseverance and frugality. Foreign broadcasts focused on undermining Nazi authority and encouraged resistance movements, such as those in France and Poland, as well as sabotage in Nazi factories.

A similar campaign followed the war when Germany was partitioned. Suddenly, the Soviet Union was the enemy, only this time the war was mostly ideological in nature with limited direct confrontation. This led to an increase in subversive activity. And as the Iron Curtain went up, the west relied heavily on print media and radio broadcasts to reach into East Berlin and beyond. The west began to use programming specifically designed to target citizens within the Soviet Union. Programs such as the Voice of America and the BCC conducted broadcasts into the USSR until about 1950, when the Soviets began jamming most (if not all) western signals. Even though western media could no longer be legally accessed, the constant jamming of non-state sources eventually led to discontent and contributed to the fall of the Soviet Union. The overt objectives of the radio broadcasts were not as successful as the west had hoped, but the Soviet reaction led to even better results. Let that serve as a lesson, that the objective can be achieved by first determining how the enemy might react.

Radio is still relevant, but its use is decreasing. In certain situations, it may still be the best option for dissemination.

4. Television

Television came shortly after radio and had an even more significant effect on discourse in the U.S. With it came a new form of storytelling, using visualization rather than vocals, and a new entertainment industry was born. Television also created a medium for journalists to broadcast news stories that could immediately reach millions. Once this happened, Americans developed strong media literacy, but it also became easier to market directly to people. As mass communication developed further, and America became more prosperous, new companies were formed specifically to spread news. During World War 2, most broadcasts revolved around entertainment and direct news from the war. However, as with radio, the intentions changed as the U.S. shifted into the Cold War. Direct conflict with the Soviets was not an option, and thus the U.S. pursued indirect paths on all fronts, including domestic and international television.

Whether they intended to or not, most broadcasters toed the official state line when reporting on events.

This attitude toward cooperation with state officials reduced slightly as the Cold War died down, but it is still common. In fact, operatives for political campaigns often intern at media-literacy organizations. Media Matters, a "media watchdog" group founded by Democratic political operative David Brock, often hosts courses for Democrat operatives to educate them about information manipulation before they go on television either as pundits or as full-time reporters. The divide between Government and Media is still very thin.

Television is a powerful medium for propaganda, but it can be difficult for outsiders to have access to it. For unconventional groups, television is rarely an option, unless direct action is taken, such as the hijacking of a TV program in Lithuania on 13 January 1991, reporting the killings of Lithuanians by Soviet Forces.

5. Internet & social media

The Internet has become the great equalizer for communication. Anyone with a connection can instantly reach thousands of people. Even in nations where the internet is restricted, groups still find ways to communicate online and expose the misdeeds of government forces. The internet also provides a significant degree of deniability through anonymity. Since it is so accessible, every modern unconventional force has a strong social media presence. ISIS, for example, used Twitter extensively to showcase the expansion of its caliphate. Its use of Twitter encouraged hundreds of Westerners to travel to Iraq and Syria to join its ranks. Its early successes also encouraged extremists in the west to commit terrorist attacks in coalition countries. ISIS took responsibility for major attacks, such as the Paris Attacks in November 2015 as well as the San Bernardino attack in December 2015. Such a global reach by a regional group was only possible through social media.

It is important to note that the anonymity of the internet works both ways. Government forces have taken advantage of it to infiltrate online groups and destabilize them or entrap them by encouraging extremist activities. Again, in the case of ISIS, France and the U.S. were able to use social media to track high-level targets. Through that tracking, the coalition air campaign was able to take out several high-level leaders as well as social media personalities and coordinators.

The internet is the most promising platform for any unconventional force to deliver its messaging. The combination of accessibility, anonymity, and reach make it extremely useful for groups who do not have the reach necessary to access television.

Symbolism is a powerful thing and using strong imagery can rally masses to any cause. Take, for example, the Soviet Hammer & Sickle. Communism has always focused on the importance of working class. In the Soviet Union, many of these people were simple peasants who worked fields or performed manual labor. The Hammer and Sickle symbol rallied millions to the communist cause because it promises power and respect, something many of those people historically lacked and desired. Many smaller communist groups have co-opted the Hammer & Sickle because of the powerful symbolism representing the global working class.

Another example is the crucifix. The crucifix existed for hundreds of years prior to the birth of Jesus Christ, and it was one of the most horrible forms of execution. Now, it is universally recognized as a positive icon, symbolizing the ultimate sacrifice of Christ. It hangs around the necks and wrists of tens millions of followers. It is the muse of tattoos, artwork, and architecture, despite its original meaning.

These forms of symbolism are rather overt and straightforward. The meaning behind them can be immediately understood, even cross-culturally. However, most symbolism is a little more abstract, and requires some understanding of psychology and sociology to fully understand.

In any given society, some things come along with generally understood connotations. Connotations serve us by providing a subconscious understanding of abstract concepts, such as colors and the emotions we assign to them (such as red being used for powerful emotions, like love, anger, or power). Therefore, good propaganda takes advantage of both the innately human and the culturally acquired subconsciousness so that it makes the viewer feel a certain way before they have a chance to fully digest the message itself. This type of covert symbolism features heavily in propaganda and is especially common in advertising. What we will call "Connotative Propaganda" can be broken down into 4 manipulatable subjects: Ego (promises of status or money), emotions (manipulation of emotions like fear or pride), patriotism (flag waving), and sex appeal (using attractive people as a prize or token).

Consider this piece of American propaganda from World War 2:

When you look at the poster, first recognize who designed it and what its purpose was. Of course, the goal is to get more men to volunteer for submarine service. But how does the propaganda go about convincing sailors that it is something they should do? Just like modern commercial advertising, the poster promises women and status. Also, take note of the colors used in the poster. Red and White feature heavily, especially on the woman's shirt, evoking the stripes on the American flag. It can be argued that the intent was to subconsciously remind the sailor that he was fighting for America, or the American women at home. The general warmth of the poster is also notable. Young men generally desire two things: purpose, and love/sex. This poster promises both. Clearly, we can see that color plays an important role in this piece specifically, but in all propaganda.

We also need to ask ourselves if this propaganda was successful in its goal, which we determined was to get more men to volunteer for submarine service. In World War 2, there were roughly 260 American submarines with 55-72 personnel per submarine, most being deployed to the pacific. Submarines alone were responsible for sinking 30% of the Japanese navy and more than 50% of all Japanese merchant vessels. Also considering the fact that staffing was never an issue and that the most successful submarines were produced almost immediately following the attack on Pearl Harbor, we can safely say that the propaganda and recruitment tactics did work.

In the modern world, the principles of propaganda still apply but the medium has changed. Now it comes in the form of mass broadcasts, social media, and corporate advertisements pandering to their audiences in the name of social causes. Everything is politicized and therefore every form of media is propaganda, you would do well to recognize this to lessen its effect on you. The Mass Media mostly uses emotional manipulation, using negatively charged words in headlines with the intent of getting the user to interact out of fear, anger, or confusion. Most mass media companies earn their revenue from corporate sponsorships and advertisements, so the more eyes they have on their content, the more money they make. From a practical business perspective, it makes sense. But it is also insidious, as many Americans (and the west in general) used to see journalism as synonymous with honesty and integrity, making them trust institutions who now publish blatant partisan falsehoods. As our society grows more divided, they benefit greatly from the turmoil.

Understanding the nature of propaganda will help you identify it and protect against it, but it will also give you the tools to disperse your own. Remember, propaganda is just a word. It is neither positive nor negative. It is not right or wrong.

Propaganda works both ways, and in an irregular conflict, having control of the narrative is key. This idea of controlling a narrative and therefore influencing the general population is critical to success in any unconventional conflict, and it is impossible to overestimate the importance of narrative.

While an unconventional group may use propaganda to convince locals that its cause is righteous and just, the enemy will use propaganda to convince them that they are evil terrorists seeking anarchy. The state propaganda machine is more developed than a guerrilla's will likely ever be. It is a network of interconnected parts working in tandem to demonize its opponents and silently slip its message into the common man's mind. A primary part of any successful counterinsurgency is turning the people against the insurgent force. They may be able to do this by convincing the public that the insurgent force's ideals are invalid or backwards. They will also use fear to convince them, threatening violence and legal punishment against anyone who supports or aids the insurgency. However, those state forces will devote an entire section of their propaganda effort to specifically targeting the insurgency, coaxing members to turn on their own people and guide state forces against them, or to simply break the will to fight. This has been a major part of all American conflicts since Vietnam, and it has been very successful.

There are ways to combat it, and successful Unconventional Groups should seek to impose a sense of discipline and camaraderie amongst its members. Without that, and a sense of confidence and fraternity, it will be disturbingly easy for state forces to sway individuals within the insurgent group to desert, inform, or sabotage. They may also direct propaganda at specific individuals. In The Malayan Emergency (a great example of a successful counterinsurgency), the British would use aircraft to broadcast messages into the vast jungles of Malaysia. They would get personal information on known communist guerrillas and play messages of their families making appeals to return home and end the conflict. It worked, and insurgents would slip out of their camps and into the night just to return a few weeks later leading a British commando group against the same people they were fighting with. They would use these same deserters to broadcast new messages begging their comrades to give up and come in, encouraging them with warm food, clean water, medical care, and, sometimes, offering pardons. This was used in Vietnam, Iraq, Afghanistan, and everywhere in between for good reason: it works, especially against forces with low morale and a weak communal identity.

Indoctrination (another negatively charged word, but one that is also neutral) should be used as often as possible. Indoctrination in this context is simply establishing a set of values and attitudes that will be followed and can be reinforced regularly. Militaries use this during basic training. In the civilian world, an appropriate synonym would be 'team building.' Without those communal values, goals, and attitudes (whether they be political, religious, or otherwise), as well as the definition of individual roles, it would be difficult to establish the bonds that will protect against propaganda efforts or the simple breakdown of group dynamics under stress.

Working, training, competing, playing, fighting, and living closely *together* can establish and strengthen those bonds. Shared experiences can create and strengthen bonds that are difficult to break. Understand what makes each other tick, and it will become possible to resist any attempt to destroy unity.

THE "DEFENSIVE FIRST STRIKE"

The opening moments of a conflict play considerable psychological roles in determining the outcome. For example, the Battles of Lexington and Concord were initiated by the British when Thomas Gage was ordered to disarm the people of Massachusetts, as the crown deemed them to be in an open state of rebellion. The aggressor was Britain and, psychologically, the aggressor is often looked at negatively. This can be seen in how the American colonies came together to form a unified response to the attacks. The Americans were attacked first but were in a position to win the first engagement due to their extensive intelligence networks throughout New England, putting them on a good footing militarily, politically, and psychologically. Many had argued that the British could not be opposed, but the swift defeat of Gage's men and the subsequent Siege of Boston proved that success was possible, and increased support for independence. Such a situation may be known as a "defensive first strike."

We can also look at the Civil War, and the Confederate attack on Fort Sumpter. The Confederates had good reason to attack the fort, as it was going to be resupplied by Union forces. Of course, the attack was an offensive action against Union forces. This had the opposite effect that the attacks on Lexington and Concord had, as it emboldened the Union in their crusade to stop the Confederacy and to re-unify the country. To highlight how important the attack was to the Union, within a month of the attack more than 110,000 Americans volunteered to put down the rebellion. By comparison, it took a year to for 161,000 Americans to volunteer after September 11th. Had the Confederacy waited and fought a defensive war, electing to pursue more guerrilla action (such as John Mosby's 43rd Virginia Cavalry), rather than continuously lashing out into Union territory and fighting pitched battles based on the Southern elite's code of gentlemanly honor, they may have won.

Allowing the opposition to strike first, while also maintaining the capability to retaliate decisively, can help a guerrilla force establish itself as a legitimate player in a conflict while also maintaining itself as an entity that is only acting in pursuit of self-preservation.

Chapter 5:

INTELLIGENCE GATHERING AND OTHER SURREPTITIOUS ACTIVITIES

"He will win who knows when to fight and when not to fight."

- ***Sun Tzu***

Intelligence is a very broad term. Even when we narrow its use down to a military context there are still numerous areas to account for. We can at least recognize that intelligence is, simply, the collection of information. That information, once acquired, is then analyzed and disseminated to the appropriate people in order to be utilized. Just like logistics, a strong intelligence gathering apparatus is mandatory for any successful fighting force, especially for guerrillas. Without it, even the most capable warfighters would not be able to find and eliminate their targets.

If we look at a military force, conventional or otherwise, as if it is a physical body, then we can picture intelligence as the nervous system, sending signals to the appropriate muscle groups and allowing them to contract as necessary. If the body did not have the nervous system, the body would be blind and motionless, unable to defend itself or understand its surroundings. This is exactly how intelligence gathering works; it acts as our eyes and ears, enabling our hands and feet to complete the tasks assigned to them by the brain.

For conventional forces, there are numerous intelligence considerations to be had, including everything from human collection to monitoring seismology and collecting geospatial information from satellites. For unconventional forces, however, the considerations are fewer just as the opportunities are fewer. Most groups do not have access to cutting-edge surveillance satellites or algorithms capable of scanning tens of millions of social media profiles, so they must make do with what they have.

For any unconventional group, knowing what the enemy is doing or capable of is the first and most pressing concern. This is where surveillance comes into play. Surveillance is the covert observation of people and groups. Surveillance can be accomplished through direct visual contact but also remotely via technology, such as listening devices, cameras, or wireless tracking tools/software (e.g., cellphones, keyloggers, and GPS trackers). These devices are fairly easy to build or obtain, especially in the west.

When it comes to in-person surveillance, it is important to do so from a position that is hidden from the view of the subject. For example, if the target is an apartment, then a neighboring apartment could be occupied to perform the surveillance. Another option would be occupying a building across the street. Regardless of where the surveillance post is established, there are two goals that need to be accomplished; 1.) gain as much information as possible and 2.) maintain cover status. If discovered, it is possible that the target will begin to intentionally feed you misleading intelligence, orchestrate an attack on the surveillance team, or they will simply abandon the location, returning you to square one. If the team is physically surveilling, the surveillance post should be close enough to effectively gather the information, but distant enough (or with enough "noise" between the post and the target) to not be suspected. The surveillance post could and, in many cases, should, be separate from the lodging or other locations relating to the cover status of the team.

A similar paradox exists with following a target in a vehicle; remain close enough so as to not lose the target, but distant enough to not be picked up. One way that this has been addressed is the use of multiple vehicles along the route. The first surveillance vehicle would be used to follow for an specified distance and as it disengages from the pursuit, another vehicle steps in to fill the void. The process would be repeated as necessary until the target reached its destination or until enough information was acquired. This requires extremely close coordination and clear communication between follow vehicles to be properly implemented, especially in an urban environment.

Another method of surveillance could be the use of informants. Planting an informant within a group or organization so as to report back information is a time-tested surveillance method. It is also highly dangerous, as it places the life and identity of the informant in jeopardy. This method requires a high level of stagecraft and improvisation, and it should be something that comes naturally to the informant. From a historical perspective, many informants who were used to infiltrate groups were thespians. These skills are extremely important for any informant and should be practiced consistently to avoid any unnecessary risks. A poorly trained informant is a liability, and thus should be avoided at all costs. If they are discovered and given the choice between death and becoming a double agent, they will likely choose the latter.

It also usually takes time and dedication for an informant to infiltrate a group and become trusted. This can take weeks, months, and sometimes years to develop the relationships necessary to yield anything of value.

RECONNAISSANCE & AREA STUDY

Reconnaissance is often used as a synonym for surveillance, but they are very different practices. While surveillance is the collection of information from observing individuals or groups and is typically passive (in that the one surveilling is waiting for information to stream in), reconnaissance is the collection of information from observing or collecting data on locations and is usually a more active, deliberate process. Reconnaissance encompasses broad topics such as geography, climate, ecology, and aspects of society. Local language, traditions, politics, and social, religious, and political institutions are all important to proper reconnaissance.

There are generally 3 types of reconnaissance:

- Force Reconnaissance
- Terrain Reconnaissance
- Civil Reconnaissance

Force reconnaissance is the observation of enemy forces; their numbers, their dispositions, their equipment, their assets (artillery, armor, aircraft, defensive installations, logistics, etc.), and their capabilities.

Terrain Reconnaissance is the study of the physical aspects of the area itself. These would be things such as mountains, forests, rivers, ridges, hilltops, and other topographical features. Other aspects would be weather, climate, and identifying features and landmarks. Terrain applies to urban areas as well and can sometimes overlap with civil reconnaissance. Examples including elevation gains and hilltops, reservoirs, canals and other waterways, etcetera.

Civil Reconnaissance is the observation of local customs, infrastructure, institutions, organizations, and beliefs. This is arguably the "densest" form of recon, as it requires you to address tangible infrastructure (e.g., bridges, airports, highways, waterworks, etc.,) as well as intangible cultural influences. Those performing civil reconnaissance can use ASCOPE (Areas, Structures, Capabilities, Organizations, People, and Events) to narrow down these factors.

A broader analysis tool that can be used for reconnaissance is PMESII-PT.

Political – Assesses the formal political power(s) and government structure in the AO as well as any informal individuals, groups, or organizations that act as political influences. Examples would include analyzing both relevant statutory and common law, systems of governance, and existing or potential political coalitions/alliances, as well as some physical locations and their compositions, such as local or regional legislatures, executive offices, courts, or other institutions.

Military – Assesses the capabilities, influence, and doctrinal standards/limitations (such as rules of engagement, SOPs, or domestic legal restrictions) of any military, paramilitary, proxy, and/or law enforcement entities.

Economic – Assesses the economic variables in an AO, including industrial capabilities, interstate/international trade, local and regional cultural economic activity, resource production/storage/consumption, resource transportation (maritime, rail, etc.) and financial management institutions.

Social – Assesses the broad cultural variables of an area, such as religious institutions & beliefs, cultural norms & taboos, racial & ethnic groups, local & regional political leanings, and any other social group/institution/belief that may contribute to a conflict in one way or another.

Information – Assesses the institutions and organizations that control the distribution or collection of information. Examples include typically benign sources, such as newspapers, news stations, or radio stations, but also more covert or malignant organizations, such as Intelligence or Law Enforcement Agencies.

Infrastructure – Assesses the various infrastructure that enable a society to function. Examples of infrastructure include dams, railroads & rail yards, highways, hospitals & clinics, bridges, airports, maritime ports, electric substations & transmission towers, cell towers, etcetera. Good analysis would also identify the resources needed to maintain and operate those structures.

Physical Environment – Assesses the various factors of the physical world, including geography (especially Physical Geography), climatology, meteorology, and the built environment.

Time – Assesses the ability to plan and/or execute decisions based on time & date restrictions or opportunities.

Additionally, it is possible to combine ASCOPE and PMESII (and PT, where applicable) to create a visual tool to assist with analysis.

	P **Political**	**M** **Military**	**E** **Economic**	**S** **Social**	**I** **Information**	**I** **Infrastructure**
A **Areas**	Voting/Congressional districts, circuit court systems, law enforcement precincts/coverage	Bases, housing, security zones	Industrial zones, markets, farms, ports	Parks, plazas, markets, campuses	TV networks, newspapers	Water access (tables, reservoirs), restricted airspace, internet coverage
S **Structures**	Local/Regional capitols, Courts, Government offices	Checkpoints, HQs, COPs	Warehouses, banks, oil rigs, factories	Churches, Bars	Cell/Radio/TV towers	Roads, bridges, dams, substations, Ports, Airports
C **Capabilities**	Conflict resolution, cooperation, legitimacy	Logistics, support units, armor/air support	Currency valuation, financing	Organizing, willingness to fight/oppose fighting	Availability of service, extent of reach/public trust	Ability to construct/maintain infrastructure, ability to support general public
O **Organization**	Parties, PACs, Social orgs, movements	Units/Chain of command	Businesses, Corporations, Banks	NGOs, Social activist groups	News stations, Intelligence Orgs	Government departments, construction companies
P **People**	Governors, senators, judges, icons/symbols	Important personnel	Businessmen, investors, bankers	Religious leaders, influential families	Company owners, news casters	Contractors, department executives, planning committees
E **Events**	Elections, council meetings, hearings	Operations, deployments, ceremonies	Droughts, War, Stock market open/close	Holidays, festivals, parades	IO campaigns, station/print openings, investigations	Construction projects, maintenance

Reconnaissance and area studies can be completed using similar frameworks and can also be completed using a combination of physical reconnaissance and open-source research.

Everything starts with reconnaissance. In fact, we can look at the beginning of just about any conflict and we can study how reconnaissance was handled by the belligerents. An example of the importance of reconnaissance would be the war planning during the Cold War. The Americans and Soviets both spent considerable time and resources reconnoitering Europe; detailing Germany, other NATO countries and, more broadly, the Great European Plain. The vast flatness of the European Plain (which stretches from parts of France in the west, to the Black Sea in the south, Kazakhstan in the East, and the Kola Peninsula in the North), is conducive to massive movements of mechanized and armored forces, which both NATO and the Soviet Union were greatly concerned about. To this day, the European Plain is a critical terrain feature and is one of the reasons Russia invaded Ukraine in February 2022., as it would be an avenue in which a hypothetical NATO or Russian invasion would occur, and control of the fertile land within the Plain would be critical to sustaining a war effort.

Continuing with the theme of NATO and Russia, we will use the ASCOPE- PMESII-PT framework to detail an example of a strategic reconnaissance of the Kola Peninsula and Murmansk Oblast, a region that faces considerable threats if war between the two powers ever broke out. In May 2022, in response to the Invasion of Ukraine and the escalating tensions between Europe and Russia, Finland's Parliament voted in favor of joining NATO. This is important because parts of Northern Russia, specifically the Kola Peninsula, lay within the European Plain. The Murmansk Oblast contains a number of critical Russian military installations including the ballistic missile early warning site in Olenegorsk, the Northern Fleet headquarters in Severomorsk which maintains most of Russia's nuclear submarines and nuclear-powered ships, ZEVS submarine communication transmitter station, as well as a number of air bases that house many of Russia's nuclear-capable long range strategic bombers. Additionally, the Murmansk Oblast is connected to the rest of Russia by only one road, the R21 highway, and one railway, Kirov railway. Due to the proximity of the Kola Peninsula to NATO (should Finland join), its strategic importance to the Russian military, and the congestion of the R21/Kirov North-South corridor, it would be one of the first targets should war break out.

Knowing these details, we can build a rough ASCOPE-PMESII-PT framework that could, potentially, assist in decision-making in a hypothetical NATO invasion of the Murmansk Oblast. Remember that this is a strategic framework designed to identify key locations and capabilities that can then enable tactical thinkers to focus on specific targets or ideas and conduct operations within the area pursuant to the strategic goal.

	P Political	M Military	E Economic	S Social	I Information	I Infrastructure
A **Areas**	Murmansk Oblast, closed cities, bases, ports	Bases, radar sites, housing, closed cities	R21 highway corridor, Murmansk Port	Parks, plazas, markets, campuses	TV-21 Murmansk, Vecherniy Murmansk newspaper	R21 corridor
S **Structures**	Local/Regional capitols, Courts, Government offices	Checkpoints, HQs, air bases, Nakhimov Naval School	Warehouses, banks, mines, factories	Churches, Stroitel Stadium, theaters	Cell/Radio/TV towers, print shops	Kola Nuclear Power plant, Murmansk Port, R21, Kirov rail, Murmansk rail station
C **Capabilities**	Ability to communicate with rest of Russia, coordinate response	Logistics, nuclear subs/LRSBs, Communication	Imports, exports, mining. Atomflot	Organizing, willingness to fight/oppose fighting	Availability of service, extent of reach/public trust	Transportation, power production, metal/mineral mining
O **Organization**	Council of Deputies, Mayor	Units/Chain of command	Businesses (SUEK, EuroChem), Banks	NGOs, Social activist groups	News stations, Intelligence Orgs	Government departments, construction companies
P **People**	Mayor, deputies, head of police	admirals of northern fleet	Businessmen, investors, bankers, Andrey Melnichenko	Religious leaders, influential families	Company owners, news casters	Contractors, department executives, planning committees
E **Events**	Elections, council meetings, hearings	Operations, deployments, ceremonies, naval school graduations		Holidays, festivals, parades	IO campaigns, station/print openings, investigations	Construction projects, maintenance

Once the strategic analysis is completed, tactical decision makers can begin to lay out more detailed reconnaissance on specific targets, using ASCOPE or similar templates to pick out specific target buildings, capabilities, and personnel. The above example is, of course, one of a potential conventional conflict, however the factors remain important for guerrillas. For example, an insurgency on the Kola peninsula might seek to sabotage the Kirov railway, as well as staging ambushes along the R21 highway, to limit the movement of resources and personnel. They might also conduct raids against isolated checkpoints and kidnappings of mid-to-high level personnel, or high-jacking communication stations to broadcast pro-insurgency messages.

Tactical analysis can be completed by using another acronym, SALT. The tactical analysis should be fed to decision makers who will then incorporate the tactical reconnaissance into their strategic planning. SALT considers the most pressing information that can be gathered from an enemy force during a reconnaissance.

Size – Refers to the size, or manpower, of the force being observed

Activity – What is the observed force doing? What is their purpose, or goal?

Location – Where is the observed force located? Are they travelling? If so, where?

Time – What time were the observations made? How long will they be there?

Example of a SALT report might be:

Salt – Estimated 1 platoon

Activity – Establishing security positions (4 checkpoints, traffic barriers, overwatch positions on the post office and the bank) and checking vehicles at checkpoints

Location – Downtown area, between 4th street and main street, with a command center in the post office

Time – 1:30 P.M.

SALT reports are the bread and butter of a reconnaissance group. Determining the size, capabilities, and activity of a potentially hostile group is key to decision making and operational planning. Multiple SALT reports will be completed under the umbrella of a strategic reconnaissance.

Once the reconnaissance element understands what to look for, they can begin to implement different types of tactical reconnaissance in order to gather that information.

There are three types of tactical reconnaissance relevant to unconventional groups:

- *Route*: The processes of reconnoitering a route. The route could be a road, highway, or trail. Routes are reconnoitered by light patrol.

- *Area*: An area reconnaissance revolves around a specific location, such as a neighborhood, valley etc., and focuses on locations of interest, such as key terrain features or buildings, as well as enemy forces and their compositions. Area reconnaissance is normally conducted via observation/listening post as well as light patrol, when necessary.

- *Zone*: Zone reconnaissance is a larger-scale reconnaissance, the bridge between the tactical and strategic-level reconnaissance. Zone reconnaissance seeks to gather as much information as possible on all terrain features, locations of interest, and enemy forces within the zone. An operating area is divided into zones.

Furthermore, these 3 types of tactical reconnaissance can be broken down into two categories:

- *Hasty*: Formed quickly with little to no notice, often by acting on newly acquired intelligence or with the intent to gather all relevant information, if any.

- *Deliberate*: Formed deliberately with an emphasis on cover and concealment, with the intent to gather very specific information on a particular subject. Can be conducted over a longer period.

Observation/Listening posts should be established in locations with sightlines to key terrain or locations. These locations are often on hilltops, mountains, or within buildings. It is important that observers do not set up their OP/LP in the most obvious or advantageous position, such as at the crest of a hilltop or the top floor/roof of a building, as that could cause the observers to *skyline* and be spotted. The OP/LP should be concealed near or below the crest, or in less-than obvious locations that still offer good sightlines to the intended target(s). The OP/LP should be constructed along the natural contours of the location, being sure to avoid any obvious non-natural shapes or patterns and should be concealed using local vegetation, when appropriate. If establishing an LP, signature emissions should be carefully observed. OPs/LPs should be conscious of any reflective materials such as skin or glass, and work to mitigate them as necessary. Scent is also a factor. Avoid cigarette usage, burning any materials (including wood), as well as the cooking of food or the use of scented deodorants. As always, any radio usage should be heavily regulated. Emissions should be short, controlled, and infrequent.

When in the process of establishing an OP/LP, or travelling between points, the observers should be continuously observing their surroundings, stopping occasionally to analyze the environment and assess potential threats or ideal OP/LP positions. Observers can use SLLS ("*sills*") to assist them in this task.

Stop – The group should stop in place to observe their surroundings

Look – The group should visually observe their surroundings. Look for signs of traffic or habitation along the path or on any nearby elevated positions

Listen – Listen for any relevant information. Is there a roadway nearby? Do aircraft pass over frequently? Do you hear voices, twigs and leaves cracking, or the sounds of a camp?

Smell – Man-made scents may be picked up easily. Perfumed deodorants or soaps, prepared food, cigarettes, and wood smoke are all signs of human activity

Additionally, groups can establish multiple LP/OP during a deliberate reconnaissance operation. *The Cloverleaf* Method, also known as *The Fan Method,* allows a team or teams to conduct active and deliberate reconnaissance on a fixed target. Bounding around the target and observing it from multiple angles, at multiple points in time, often creates a Cloverleaf shape around the fixed objective. This method can provide a holistic understanding of the target. Of course, the purpose of all intelligence gathering is to generate the most useful, relevant, and up-to-date information for decision makers, and The Cloverleaf Method enables observers to accomplish this aim. It is also worth mentioning that a perfect cloverleaf shape will not always appear, as the routes taken are entirely dependent on the proclivities of opposing forces and any restrictive or advantageous terrain.

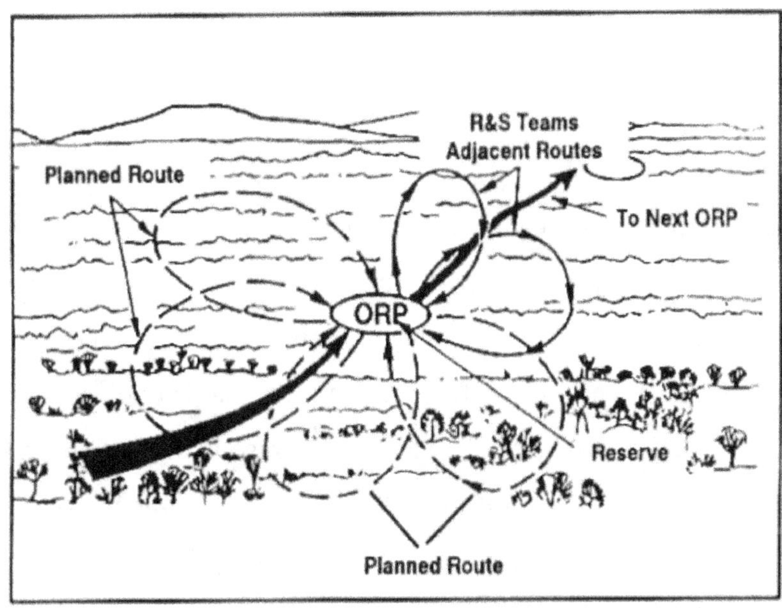

Figure 4-6. Fan method.

Another important aspect of reconnaissance, particularly for unconventional forces, is, if operating in an urban less-than permissive civilian environment, those doing the recon should be able to blend in. A New Yorker would stick out in rural Georgia, but not necessarily in Atlanta. A Sikh man would stick out in Tralee, but not in London. Again, referencing the War in Afghanistan, special forces and cultural attaches would often dress in local garb, use local transportation, speak the local language, and learn cultural norms and taboos to better blend in and respect the locals. This was often a better approach to gathering local and regional information than storming into a village with an armed convoy and dragging people out of their *qalʿahs* by their hair. The awareness and understanding of factors such as race, gender, linguistics, politics, religion, appearance, and how the various groups in a particular area interact is paramount. If those doing the reconnaissance do not look, sound, or act like they belong where they are, then they will attract unnecessary attention.

Reconnaissance is necessary for conventional forces and unconventional groups alike. Every group should seek to understand its area of operation (down to the most minute detail) long before it must wage a war in it.

Sabotage has always been among the first choices of action for every unconventional force. When facing an enemy with massive supply lines and a heavy reliance on regularly delivered supplies, sabotage can be extremely effective when a smaller, objectively weaker force is up against a large, lumbering conventional force. The goal is not just to commit the sabotage, but to accomplish a longer-term goal, such as to drain resources and manpower, or to cause troop movements to be diverted. For example, the WWII Belgian *Groupe G* was a sabotage group of mostly engineering students and professors who ingeniously attacked roads, bridges, and knocked out entire electric networks. These actions caused the Germans to spend a considerable amount of time and resources on repairing and guarding the infrastructure, all resources that could have otherwise gone to the war effort against the allies.

Sabotage has been prevalent in every conflict, and if done correctly, can yield impressive results. Germany committed many acts of sabotage in New York prior to America's direct involvement in World War 1, attacking piers, railyards, and ammunition plants in the hopes of reducing support for the Entente. In the attack on a munitions depot on Black Tom Island, German agents were placed within the area and offered bribes to security guards, who then allowed the agents access to place small charges and incendiary devices throughout the arms depot. While the sabotage did the opposite of the intended effect, it still levied considerable psychological stress against Americans, and especially New Yorkers.

Operation Jaywick, executed by only six men, led to the surprise destruction of six Japanese shipping vessels in the harbor of Singapore using simple limpet mines and canoes. Additionally, during the 2003 invasion of Iraq, the Kurds sabotaged train lines and power stations in Iraq, not necessarily to stop trains or kill electricity access in cities, but to draw some of the Iraqi army away from other strategic objectives that American forces intended to target. Sabotage does not need to be done just for the sake of sabotage, as it can assist in the accomplishment of other objectives, nor does it need to be done on a grand, strategic level. It can be done locally on a smaller scale, so long as it serves to harass or wear down the conventional force and accomplish strategic goals.

Anything can be subject to sabotage. Production is especially attractive to would-be saboteurs as it directly supplies enemy forces. Munition plants are prime targets in every conflict. Sometimes, workers within the plant may surreptitiously plant charges on key equipment or within storage areas. Other targets include infrastructure, such as ports, military communication networks, and railways. Infrastructure targets could also be oil refineries, warehouses, and even banks. Anything that may interrupt normal function of the facility may be subject to targeting (port cranes, pipelines, cell towers, etc.,) Typically, guerrillas will avoid putting undue stress on the public, such as attacking locations that offer critical services or consumer goods, such as gas stations or supermarkets, which would only make it more difficult for them to acquire basic goods, and therefore will sap support from the public.

Being able to infiltrate a non-permissive location is something that can yield great information and opportunities. Doing so can serve many purposes and is especially useful for saboteurs and intelligence gatherers. Some of the skills used during reconnaissance are applicable here, such as "looking the part" and blending in. Infiltration is also a career field for some. Physical Penetration Testers, also sometimes known as red teams, are often hired by companies and governments to find physical security flaws in installations, offices, warehouses, or research & development centers. These professional intruders use social engineering and various types of technology (both low and high-tech) to infiltrate skyscrapers, water treatment plants, and electrical substations with an objective defined by them and their client, such as gaining access to a specific area or planting a fake bug in a board room. These red teams find ways to defeat various security systems, such as RFID badge readers, FLIR cameras, mantraps, and motion sensors.

Oftentimes, access to a secure building is as simple as looking the part. Dressing like a maintenance man or a housekeeper (with the associated props and/or identification) can help someone gain access to a building. Certain mass-produced keys for things like public elevators, filing cabinets, handcuffs, apartment security boxes, and Ford Crown Victoria's can be purchased online. Some keys can offer entry to a location, while others can completely lock a location down, such as the 1620 Fireman key. When the only obstacle is a locked door (without a deadbolt), then it is possible to pick the door and have access. Effective physical security is often an afterthought to cyber security, especially in older buildings, and with the right amount of reconnaissance on a potential target, almost anyone can infiltrate the location.

A building may be fortified with multiple layers of security, preventing access to certain areas from certain approaches. However, these security layers are often superficial. That is, there may be a deadbolt on a door, but the walls of the adjoining room(s) may consist of little more than drywall and framing. In this aspect, some criminals could be considered geniuses (at least for the purposes of entering structures), as many burglaries begin through indirect entry points. Some dig tunnels under the site, mapping out city pipes and wiring to avoid accidents or utility interruptions that would warrant attention from authorities (such was the case of the LA-based

Hole in the Ground Gang). Others go in through the roof, using ventilation shafts, skylights, or unalarmed emergency exits. Burrowing through the wall, especially if there is a connected building with less security than the actual target, is also an option. Other times, security may not be a considerable factor at all, and the only obstacle between a person and their target may be an unelectrified fence. Such was the case of the Brussels Airport Diamond Heist, in which a group of gunmen got away with over $50 million in diamonds (though many, but not all, were later caught, tried, and acquitted) by simply hiding in an unoccupied construction site adjacent to the airport and then cutting through a chain link fence. They also used vehicles with police markings to assist them in getting close to escape from their target.

Additionally, when lacking finesse or other options, brute force can sometimes be the solution. In June 2022, over a dozen armed men broke into a private freight yard near the Port of Manzanillo, Colima, Mexico, and escaped with 20 shipping containers filled with partially refined silver, gold, televisions, and other high-end electronics. Some estimates placed the value of the containers at several billion dollars. Using speed, surprise, and violence of action, the gunmen broke into their target and subdued the armed guards before any shots were fired and maintained their cover for over eight hours. Additionally, they had the intelligence to identify the correct containers as well as their contents. They also had the technical knowledge to manipulate container cranes and the logistical capability to load the containers onto a convoy of trucks before escaping into the interior of Colima.

Even burglars have lessons to teach about infiltrating targets. Most buildings have distinct human patterns that can be identified. What routes do security guards follow on their patrols, or are they static? When does the armored truck arrive to collect cash? What methodology do maids use when cleaning rooms? What about Maintenance men? What times to employees go on breaks, and what doors do they use? When do they come back? Do they use RFID keycards? How could one procure such a key, or create a copy of one? These are just a few of the questions that a decent burglar could ask when casing a location. Workers follow patterns, and, especially in settings with highly regimented lifestyles such as those in the corporate world, those patterns can be easily identifiable. It simply takes a degree of attention and patience. Once the patterns are identified, one can begin to look at how the site can be accessed.

There is a limit, of course, to what can be infiltrated. A major military base or government building will be exponentially more secure than a rural police station or a hotel. Consider not only the factors within the target itself, but also the surrounding areas. Is the area heavily populated? Is it wilderness, with difficult terrain or open ground? Is it a densely populated urban or peri-urban environment? What is the distance/response time of local law enforcement? Is the local population older or younger? Are there schools, hospitals, or other locations nearby that would warrant an increased law enforcement/surveillance presence? What time of the day has the least amount of activity? Are there night guards? What avenues of escape are available, and which of those might be locked down, and how quickly? Mundane topics like urban planning, economics, and even racial or socioeconomic demographics play a role in planning. These are only a few of the concerns that should be addressed before any action is taken.

SOCIAL ENGINEERING

Social Engineering is the use (or abuse) of human psychology to gain access to sensitive or classified information or locations. Oftentimes when we hear about social engineering, it involves phone or email-based scammers trying to trick gullible people out of money or personal information. However, not all social engineers are foreign "princes" trying to get their inheritance. Again, red teamers are involved in this area and have done quite a bit to expand our understanding of both infiltration as well as human psychology. They still use the phone calls that scammers love, known as "vishing," but their methods expand into every field, including emails (phishing), text messages (smishing), and, of course, physical infiltration.

A large part of social engineering is understanding and taking advantage of social psychology and sociology. Most people, especially in the west, recognize some degree of authority and trust. The roles social engineers take on may already have an aura of authority and trustworthiness, such as a coworker from another team or from human resources (known as pretexting). Social Engineers also use urgency, frustration, sadness, and fear to activate the empathy or sympathy of the target, increasing the likelihood of success. To further this end, studies have shown that female social engineers enjoy more success due to the societal desire to help women, especially among men (damsel in distress).

Some examples of a potential attack would be a person from the IT department calling to warn you about a virus going around the company and requesting that you to provide them your computer login information or ask to physically borrow your laptop. They would use urgency and fear to accomplish this, and alert you to the potential consequences of allowing a virus to spread through the company system, consequences that *you* would be responsible for. A similar situation can occur when they ask to borrow your phone to make a phone call.

Another example would be a stranger standing outside of a keycard-restricted door and waiting for someone with clearance to open the door, going either in or out, and using an excuse to justify their ambling, if asked ("I left my key at my desk/in my car/at home"). This is called piggybacking, and is used quite frequently in corporate settings, as people tend to want to be helpful and non-confrontational. Sometimes, when red teams enter a target, they can wander around for hours before anyone, security or otherwise, questions them. Only certain types of people would stop to question the stranger or outright deny them entry without a keycard of their own. This social rule may change if the location in question has heightened security measures or if it engages in sensitive work.

Finally, physical penetration testers can defeat security systems such as FLIR cameras by using paintballs, spraying aerosol on the lens, or using a large pane of glass to simply walk past the camera (while impractical, this technique has been used). Also, for one-way motion-sensing doors, such as those in hospitals, penetration testers may use aerosol cans to shoot a cloud through a gap in the frame and into the view of the motion sensor, thus opening the door. To defeat human security, they may simply don clothing and equipment that will rouse little attention, such as dressing like a maintenance man in a hotel or at a construction site.

These are only a few of the solutions that have been used, and penetration testers are constantly finding unique and clever solutions to security questions because of their curiosity.

HUMINT (Human Intelligence), SIGINT (Signals Intelligence), and OSINT (Open-Source Intelligence) are the most accessible intelligence gathering disciplines available to unconventional forces.

- Human Intelligence is intelligence derived from human sources, such as defectors, captured forces, civilians, and AOIs.
- Signals Intelligence is intelligence derived from electronic signals, such as those from radios or other signal-emitting equipment, like aircraft.
- Open-Source Intelligence is intelligence derived from open sources, such as the internet, social media, public records, and newspapers.

These disciplines do not typically require any specialized equipment, and even SIGINT can be gathered from simple home-made or store-bought technology, like SDRs (Software Defined Radio) and antennas.

In fact, most disciplines are accessible to unconventional forces in some fashion, but can be very . For example, groups can use GEOINT (Geospatial Intelligence), but the available information may be restricted to publicly available satellite data that may not be the most accurate or up to date. Sources for GEOINT include the USGS Earth Explorer and Sentinel's Open Access Hub. Additionally, groups can utilize drones to create their own maps with a considerable degree of accuracy. MASINT (Measurement and Signature Intelligence), is used to gather visual or auditory measurements that the naked eye might not be able to detect. An example of MASINT collection could be a FLIR camera on a game trail, an acoustic device on an armored vehicle tracking incoming sniper fire, and doppler radars tracking storms. MASINT is a broad discipline and can be done with highly advanced technology or simple, publicly available methods and tools.

HUMINT, however, is often the most common discipline used for guerrilla forces. HUMINT can be gathered by simply conversing with or observing humans, and gathering intelligence based on the direct information they give, or by the way they act. HUMINT handlers should know how to question individuals using tact, as the direct approach may not always yield relevant or useful information. Engaging with and intentionally listening to an interviewee is often a rewarding approach, and there are several techniques out there, focusing on a variety of approaches. Human intelligence is also gathered from the classic handler-agent relationship found in traditional espionage. These handler-agent relationships are almost always transactional. It is important to remember that both sides of such a relationship are based on opportunity, and are rarely, if ever, based on goodwill.

These types of HUMINT gathering operations are always initiated by a handler and an agent coming together. The first interaction can be initiated by the handler, the prospective agent, or a third party. It goes without saying that any interaction between the agent, handler, and/or third party should be conducted in a manner that is situation appropriate. Based on known and unknown factors, the handler should take measures and precautions to protect their own life, the life of the agent, as well as the potential status of the relationship. For example, it may be appropriate to meet in public, other cases not so much. Also, the taking and/or encouraging of risk should be appropriate and not be careless. The handler should be morally, ethically, and intellectually mature enough before making any calls that deviate from normal procedures.

These handler-agent relationships are initiated and maintained by taking advantage of motivations, a collection of goals, desires, or beliefs that must be present in order to make the partnership work. These motivations can be summarized by using MICE-RC:

- Money
- Ideology
- Compromise
- Ego
- Revenge
- Coercion

Each motivation is driven by emotion, and as we saw in Chapter 4, emotions can be used to control and manipulate the conscious and subconscious mind. Motivations should always be viewed from the prospective agent's point of view, in an attempt to fully understand their motivations before engaging with them in any meaningful way.

Additionally, to better help us understand each of these motivations, we can divide them into one of two categories: *Intrinsic* (coming from internal motivations), and *Extrinsic* (coming from external motivations). Intrinsic motivations are generally more stable and less pliable to manipulation and are therefore more reliable. Extrinsic motivations stem from what can be gained or controlled and are in an inherent state of flux that can be easily manipulated, therefore making them less reliable.

MONEY

At first glance, you might believe a desire for money stems from simple greed, which is sometimes true. However, we all need money to live, to buy food, to keep our families cared for, and sometimes, to escape to safety. Money, and all that it can grant, is integral to the lives of most people. It directly impacts their comfort and opportunities. Consider Earl Pitts, a former FBI Special Agent, who fed classified information to the Soviet Union for 5 years in return for money. Part of his motivation was the fact that he felt he was being humiliated by the FBI. At the time of his spying, he lived in New York City and made $25,000 annually (roughly $51,000 today), a salary he believed was not enough for a good standard of living in the city. He was also still making student loan payments for his college education, adding further financial burden. His poor standard of living, which is entirely determined by *his* perception of what the "standard" should have been, was not being met by the FBI and he believed it was an intentional slight. Other motivations, namely Revenge and Ego, played a large role in his recruitment, as he was angry at the FBI for not paying him more and for not respecting him or his contributions. While it could be argued that Pitts' motivation was greed, it is more nuanced than that, as most things are. *He* believed he was worth more and deserved more. He was not getting that value from the FBI and the KGB offered what he was looking for. Ironically, the KGB handler was eventually turned and ended up giving Pitts back to the FBI. Once Pitts' motivations are understood (or even before they were understood, when he would make complaints or ask for loans), one can cross-reference them with Abraham Maslow's *Hierarchy of Needs* and easily see how Pitts could have turned. Understanding who you are working with is a critical function of any partnership. Money would be an extrinsic motivator.

Ideology is used when the prospective agent believes in something greater than themselves. It is usually a set of ideals and convictions that a person believes in. Ideology can be broad, and can include personal politics, preferred economics, religious beliefs, and more. An example of ideology driving an agent would be, perhaps, an individual informing against an existing regime because the regime has become corrupt, or it goes against their fundamental, religious, or personal values. They are seeking to better their society (again, the goal is to understand motivations from all perspectives), by providing information. Ideology is an intrinsic motivator, as the individual is acting based on established beliefs, morals, and ideas that form who they are.

Compromise is when the handler and the agent meet halfway, providing something to each other in a symbiotic way, summarized as "Do me this favor and I'll do something for you." The agent could be in trouble financially or is being investigated and is at risk of being caught. The agent might provide information to a foreign intelligence service in return for being smuggled out of harm's way or for money. Perhaps the potential agent has a family member in need for medical care and is willing to cooperate in return for their treatment. In a way, all handler-agent relationships feature compromise in some way. Utilizing compromise is to understand the wants and needs of the potential agent and finding a way to offer them that need, while also balancing the value of that need with the degree of risk they are taking. Like all motivations, if the risk outweighs the reward, then the agent has the potential to be turn. The opposite is also true, in that if the reward is too great, the agent may take unnecessary risks. Compromise is an extrinsic motivator, as the factors influencing the agent are external to their person.

Ego is the sense of importance we believe we have. On Maslow's Hierarchy of Needs, Ego is found in Esteem and Self-Actualization. Ego directly ties into the human's sense of value and identity. When an individual feels as though their allies or their organization no longer respect the individual's contributions, efforts, or potential, they may feel inclined to turn against them and begin informing in order to achieve or re-gain a sense of importance, self-respect, or value. If an organization is unable or unwilling to serve or provide value to its own people, it should be expected that those people will seek out other ways to acquire their needs. Consider, again, Earl Pitts. He not only believed he needed more money to make it in New York City, but he also felt disrespected and unappreciated by the FBI. His Ego had been slighted and he demanded better for himself. Ego is an intrinsic motivator.

REVENGE

Revenge, like Ideology, can be a very strong motivator. Revenge is applicable when a prospective agent feels like they, or someone they love, have been wronged or violated and the agent seeks to right or "un-do" the wrong. The desire for revenge is rooted in deep, primal human emotions. It can fuel a person for an entire lifetime. A handler offering an agent the opportunity for revenge can create a motivated force capable of anything. However, a man motivated by revenge can be unpredictable and violent. Handlers working with agents bent on revenge may elect to draw closer to the agent or "reign them in" in order to better understand them, gauge their stability, and control them. Revenge is an intrinsic motivator.

COERCION

Coercion is a motivator that should be avoided, if at all possible, as it creates a degree of enmity between the handler and the agent. Historically, handlers have used coercion by kidnapping or holding the agent's family, freezing their assets, and threatening them with prison or execution. When faced with these threats, the agent will often begrudgingly obey. Additionally, handlers may forge or acquire blackmail that could ruin the social or political standing an individual has, or they may simply This type of relationship could trigger another motivator for the agent, Revenge or Ego. Using coercion could induce the agent to seek aid from another power, hoping to find a way to free themselves from the handler while also regaining control of whatever was being used as leverage. Again, coercion as a motivator should be avoided unless it is a last resort and/or the agent can be closely monitored and controlled. Coercion is an extrinsic motivator.

Niccolò Machiavelli accurately described the fickle nature of man in his work *The Prince*. He identified us as covetous, ungrateful, and nasty creatures. He took an antipathetic stance when it comes to his fellow man, and he is not far off, especially in the realm of HUMINT. The reality is that when stakes are involved, humans will almost always do what is in their own self-interest, or the interest of those they care about. Sometimes those self-interest can involve helping others, but in the end, they are usually self-serving. Any individual is susceptible to any of the intrinsic or extrinsic motivators, and their allegiances can change at any time based on several factors. While HUMINT may oftentimes be the fastest way to gain information, it is rarely the most reliable, and intelligence received should always be cross-referenced with other sources to confirm its veracity. Any time a handler is given the opportunity to recruit an agent, they should check extensively the potential agent's bona fides, to guarantee that they have the access or capability they claim to have, while also safeguarding against infiltrators and informants. Additionally, some intelligence agencies have had a history of handlers getting too close to their agents, becoming (what they believed to be) friends, or even becoming involved romantically or sexually, only to be tricked out of information by the agent who had been turned by another party. This should be avoided at all costs, as it endangers all parties, the mission, and the flow of information. The handler may frame the relationship as a friendship or partnership if it assists them in developing the agent, but the handler should always maintain control and take great care not to become too close to an agent.

Beyond the use of espionage and the handler-agent relationship, information can also be gathered from locals by asking about their observations. They may work in an office building near a port, or perhaps they live next to an airport, or along a highway. Observations from these people could be useful. Like all sourced information, any information from such sources should be cross-vetted as thoroughly as possible without losing the initiative and surprise effect that the intelligence might grant.

SIGINT, however, has historically been the one of the most reliable sources of gathering intelligence. Signals intelligence can be gathered from the interception and monitoring of signals emitted from radios, aircraft, radars, weapon systems, and any other signal-emitting technology. SIGINT can be a very technical discipline, as there are several factors at play, from antenna type to atmospheric and solar conditions. Intercepting radio traffic is a primary source of SIGINT and is almost always actively pursued (though encryption is an obstacle and will be discussed in a later section). Additionally, SIGINT does not apply only to military-scale technology. It is also common for aircraft, civilian vehicles, and public transit to use transmitters and receivers that enable Wi-Fi and GPS, which can be identified, accessed, monitored, and sometimes manipulated. Cell phones, of course, continuously give off signals (even when shut off or placed in Airplane mode) and can be used to track a person's physical location. Observing any these signals may be done by using a waterfall display, which visualizes the signals across a given spectrum. One way a person can access a waterfall display is by using an SDR (Software Defined Radio). SDRs can *modulate* (encode information) and *demodulate* (extract information) from transmitted radio signals. In contested environments, all forces will likely have access to tools that can gather and parse through SIGINT. It is critical that users engage signal management to limit all emitted signals. Being brief and concise when emitting, as well as using other tools and SOPs to reduce or spread-out emissions (such as comms windows) will help reduce an opponent's SIGINT capabilities. Using Radio Direction Finding, any signal can be identified and tracked if emitted for too long or too frequently from the same location. SIGINT is as accessible as it is dangerous, and groups around the world are beginning to implement

SIGINT into their intelligence gather repertoire. It is a complex subject that takes plenty of study, time, and investment to develop into a hard skill. It is a skill, however, that is critical to any force in the 21st century.

Finally, there is OSINT, which can be gathered from any open source, such as the internet. OSINT has been neglected by the intelligence community in the past, but in recent years has become a bigger focus, especially for police departments. Consider the amount of data that the average person shares online today. They share their locations, and while they are there, they record their surroundings. The photos they share often contain metadata than can be mined, and useful information can then be extracted. During the riots in the United States throughout 2017 and 2021, almost all major events could be tracked real-time via social media. Law enforcement and anyone following along at home could watch events unfold and track which group was where via Twitter and the livestreams on periscope, Instagram, and Facebook. Additionally, Snapchat's Snap Map (a live heat map of snaps being posted) was used to track where the bulk of protesters and rioters were going. Individuals participating in the protests and riots online discovered that privacy was an illusion, and began doxing individuals they disagreed with, releasing their names, places of work, home addresses, and other critically private pieces of information, and weaponized it all to wreak havoc on their lives. Additionally, OSINT does not always need to be collected manually, as there are very powerful OSINT tools available for those who know how to use them, such as Maltego, Shodan, SpiderFoot, and theHarvester. These tools can help reveal information that is hidden below the surface of the internet we can see. They can also help sort through the incomprehensible amount of information that can be gathered from online sources, most of which is completely useless to investigations. They help parse through billions of open sources and help identify links between subjects, or by identifying connected devices,

Counterintelligence is the act of countering, circumventing, or deceiving efforts of hostile intelligence networks. In a counterinsurgency, intelligence gathering takes a front row seat. Without the use of timely and accurate intelligence, it is not possible for a conventional force to track and eliminate insurgents, nor is it possible for them to counter any non-military efforts. The same is true for the insurgents themselves. The insurgent is aware that intelligence gathering is usually the priority for a counterinsurgency program, so the insurgent will actively seek to disrupt intelligence gathering efforts. In doing so, they reduce the effectiveness of conventional forces that seek to kill them or limit their influence. Without intelligence, there is very little to act on. Additionally, by insurgents implementing effective counterintelligence, it is possible that the conventional forces may lose faith or trust in their intelligence capabilities, further decreasing effectiveness and creating mistrust among them.

One way that unconventional groups have increased their counterintelligence efficiency is compartmentalization. Compartmentalization is the restriction of sensitive information to a select group of people. This not only restricts who has access to the information (therefore creating a smaller pool of individuals to investigate if information IS leaked), but also takes away the opportunity for lower-level individuals to leak information accidentally or voluntarily. Compartmentalization can be used on the strategic level all the way down to the mission level, with a commander or a team leader waiting until the very last moment to share the mission, objectives, or other mission-sensitive details. This secrecy should be used sparingly. If it becomes the norm, then the culture of secrecy could make lower-level individuals feel as though they are not trusted, potentially leading to a decrease in unit cohesion. Worst case, it could push a normally trustworthy person to share information with the enemy (review the list of motivators in the HUMINT section). Compartmentalization is a strong tool, but it should be used intelligently.

Another way to minimize intelligence threats is operational security (OPSEC). As mentioned earlier, it is not uncommon for people to document every moment of their day. Taking pictures of surroundings, carrying cell phones, fitness tracking watches, or other devices that regularly emit signals or upload GPS data, and telling friends or spouses where/when/why they are going somewhere are all examples of OPSEC violations. Strong OPSEC prevents bits of information from leaking out. Intelligence analysts thrive on these little pieces of the puzzle and are patient enough for those pieces to come out one by one. Eventually, if enough pieces leak, they can put together the puzzle. Restrict radio usage to specific times or events, what is shared online, details given to others, and use vague or coded language when not in private environments.

Counterintelligence is not entirely defensive. If an unconventional group becomes aware of an intelligence operation against them, instead of completely shutting down operations, they can begin to feed the hostile operation false information (this can be countered again, however, and be fed false information themselves). This deception, when used correctly and sparingly, can be used to set up ambushes and create misdirection, something guerrilla forces should be especially adept at. By feeding false information, guerrilla forces can potentially cast doubt on what information the hostile intelligence operation had previously obtained. This doubt can become paralytic for the hostiles, causing indecision amongst leaders, or encouraging urgency that could cause a misstep.

INTERROGATION, TORTURE, AND ESCAPE

In any conflict, interrogation and torture will be used. It is unavoidable. Prisoners of War will be gathered and abused until the information they have within them is exposed. Then, when the detainee is bled dry of their usefulness, they will either be cast into a cell or killed. Recently, in the Global War on Terror, Intelligence agencies have been given a wide berth when it comes to extrajudicial detention and torture (sometimes called "enhanced interrogation"). The CIA alone has established numerous "black sites" across the globe, facilities where HUMINT specialists can safely torture detainees without interruption or consequence. These sites are often hidden in Eastern Europe (Poland, Hungary, Romania), Southeast Asia (Thailand, Cambodia, Philippines), and Africa (Egypt, Morrocco, Djibouti).

Of course, interrogation is also used by ordinary police, simply looking for information or inconsistencies a suspect may reveal in a series of interviews after detention. However, even police use fear, discomfort, threats, and psychical violence to coax information (whether it be false or not) out of suspects. Police developed the Reid Technique, or the "good cop, bad cop" technique, which is now used across global police forces as well as in the intelligence community. Unconventional groups can and should learn to identify some of the tactics used by interrogators to withhold as much sensitive information as possible. Torturers, however, typically resort to horrendous tactics to abuse the detainee. It is extremely difficult to withstand some of the tactics they may resort to, but not impossible.

Consider Henri Alleg, a communist journalist in French Algeria. Alleg was eventually arrested by French Paratroopers for his anti-colonial reporting. During his detention, he would be sexually humiliated, beaten, and electrocuted. He was waterboarded and his genitals were burned and electrocuted. His ears, his throat, and his nipples would also become targets for the electricity and fire. They would repeat these patterns for days. They left him to completely dehydrate and starve in the Algerian heat. When the physical harm did not break him, the paratroopers resorted to psychological harm. They threatened his wife and children (both of whom were still in France), saying that they had been captured and were going to be executed as well. They threatened his friends and acquaintances in France and Algeria. They made it seem like at any moment he could be executed, with soldiers preparing false executions and then abruptly leaving the room. They had men and women screaming in neighboring rooms, some he thought were his friends and wife. They sent in new soldiers who were kind, in the hope of tricking him into thinking that the torture was over and convince him to divulge information. These new soldiers fed him and provided water, giving him a temporary comfort, only for the torturers to return and go right back to the abuse when Alleg still did not talk. They even resorted to using the "truth drug," Sodium Pentothal, to coerce him into talking. Even this did not work. If an average man like Henri Alleg can withstand it, anyone can.

Other tools that have been used on detainees include playing extremely loud music or disturbing sounds for sustained periods of time, "pressure positions" or being packed into small boxes, extreme sleep deprivation, being stripped naked before other men, tooth and nail extractions, sexual violence and humiliation between men, and many other methods. If the detainee is offered food, but refuses, the detainer may force-feed the detainee with a calorie-dense liquid slurry to keep the detainee from starving.

The goal for any combatant that has been detained is to retain as much information as possible from the interrogators for as long as possible. The detainee must realize that torture is, at its core, a form of reinforcement training. Any animal can be trained to follow commands, so long as positive and negative reinforcements are given. The training is a series of positive and negative reinforcements intended to illicit a response. When they torture, they mean to make the detainee uncomfortable enough to reveal information, while the detainee is hoping to alleviate the discomfort. When they provide comforts or reprieve, they do it to convince the detainee that they are, ultimately, good, or that there is a way to end the torture. If they are dehydrating a detainee, they will dangle a glass of water in front of them, offering the contents of the glass for the contents of the detainee's mind. For some people, this is an easy trade. They do this to activate base human emotions and physiological responses, fight or flight. It is possible to resist by embracing the pain and realizing that the tortures will never be the detainees' friends, or by focusing on one's own convictions. Dwelling on the fact that, ultimately, any information divulged will only go towards harming one's comrades and, therefore, aiding the same people that are committing the torture, could also help. The detainers may provide food, a blanket, some water, but they only do it because they know that this could break the detainee and give them what they want, not because they are kind. Detainees should remember that they will not be released by capitulating, they will only be complicit in the capture or killing of their allies. IF the detainee IS released, it is for one of two reasons: 1) To treat the detainee as a "Judas" that will inadvertently lead the detainers back to the rest of the group, or 2) With the goal of the detainee becoming an informant.

Being able to detect patterns and understand motives is another way to resist, as understanding what drives the interrogator/torturer to choose their methods and strategies takes away some degree of their power. Finding ways to take and keep small bits of power or control in a situation in which the detainer hopes to rob them of all control can help the detainee resist mentally. The detainee should also remind themselves constantly what, and who, they are fighting for. The tortures will seek to make the detainee forget everything outside of the immediate situation. No matter what action is taken by the detainee, the pain will be unavoidable. It would have to be withstood until the body and mind are no longer capable of withstanding the violence. It is up to the detainee to decide if they intend to last as long as they can, hoping for rescue or release, or to die in captivity with their secrets retained.

Contrary to Alleg's experiences, however, there are methods that can extract information that do not constitute physical or psychological torment. Hanns Scharff was a German Luftwaffe interrogator who did not use torture to interrogate detainees. Instead, he would use slight discomforts (such as the disorientation that a new detainee experiences upon arrival to the detention site) in order to coax them into revealing bits of information at a time. Scharff would provide comforts such as warm food, medical care, and sometimes alcohol, that would make the detainee feel as though Scharff was an ally, or, at the very least, that he truly cared for their wellbeing. Detainees were also given an unprecedented degree of freedom, given their positions, to wander the grounds and go on local excursions with chaperones. As the divide between friend and foe was muddied, the detainee would slowly begin to reveal more and more information, helping Scharff fill the gaps in his knowledge. Following the war, numerous German officers and scientists were brought to the United States, including Scharff, who spent years conducting lectures on his interrogation methods, speaking to the Pentagon, an array of colleges, and at psychology conferences. To this day, his methods are studied and applied by police, military HUMINT units, and psychologists.

Torture itself is not that effective in achieving its goal, and it is why it is being used less and less (that is not to say that it is uncommon by any means). Torture is not a good way to get accurate information from a clear mind. Torture has, historically, been only for the sake of torture. ISIS fighters did not mock and harass Iraqi civilians before burning and drowning them alive in cages because they needed information, they did it because they were sadistic, evil creatures. Medieval European societies did not develop horrible torture methods such as the thumb screw or the blood eagle because they were effective at coaxing out reliable information, they were used, more often than not, as a punishment for crimes, noncompliance, or dishonor. Today, it is more common that interrogators will make the detainee uncomfortable psychologically. They may even provide comforts to draw the detainee closer, as Scharff did. Both torture and interrogation have had successes and failures, but as new conflicts spark and old ones die out, we can see how some methods work and others do not. After all, Henri Alleg did not break.

The goal for any captured individual, however, should be to escape captivity and return to the fight as soon as possible. The shorter the period in captivity, the less likely information will be given to the detainers. Escapees should remember to avoid panic or despair, and focus on coming up with a solid plan, envisioning success, and then executing.

Oftentimes, when in detention (especially in military situations), communication between two prisoners is heavily regulated specifically to avoid any kind of cooperation. Looking for gaps in such security and then finding ways to communicate, such as with written notes or morse code, could assist in coordination. Sudden, mass actions conducted with speed and extreme violence of action could lead to a successful escape, as was the case with the 1983 Batticaloa Prison escape in Sri Lanka. After communicating the plan and hiding such communications from guards, a number of coordinated groups consisting of political prisoners and members of the Tamil Tigers (a Sri Lanka-based militant group) attacked, overwhelmed, and detained guards. None of the guards were killed. This coordinated action allowed 41 of them to escape, most finding security in the Tamil Tigers' stronghold of north-eastern Sri Lanka or by leaving the island via boat for the south-Indian state of Tamil Nadu.

Additionally, prisoners could escape from captivity with help from the outside. In times of conflict, prisons are often hastily constructed or small in scale, sometimes consisting only of brittle walls, guards, and barbed wire. Militant groups take advantage of this by attacking prisons to break out prisoners and then re-integrating them into the fight. In 2008, the Taliban conducted a direct attack against the Sarposa Prison in Kandahar, Afghanistan. They began by using a VBIED (vehicle-borne improvised explosive device) to destroy the main gate, followed by a sending in a number of small teams into the prison to engage security forces and release prisoners. Meanwhile, other fighters commandeered local busses and civilian vehicles to transport released prisoners out of the city.

Groups could also enable escape, rather than directly breaking prisoners out. The IRA conducted such a breakout in 1983 at the infamous maximum security prison *Long Kesh*.

Undercover IRA operatives were able to work as security guards within the prison and report on the internal security and layout of the prison. Firearms and tools were also smuggled into the prison. Additionally, it was planned that escape vehicles and armed support would be available at the exact moment that the prisoners escaped, but that plan was derailed due to time constraints and most of the escapees had to secure their own means of escape. The prisoners, using the smuggled firearms and makeshift knives, used violence of action and were able to overpower the guards in their cell block and take over other parts of the prison, eventually getting to the guard house and main gate.

Prison breaks are extremely difficult tasks to undertake. The location is often hardened with multiple layers of security, including armed guards, multi-layer fences, cameras, and motion sensors, and local police/military response teams. These operations require extensive reconnaissance and tradecraft to successfully execute and are still daunting due to the sheer number of factors involved. It would often be most appropriate to liberate any captured individuals while they are in transit, rather than waiting until they have been delivered to a hardened holding site. Even this would require pre-planning and intelligence gathering to identify the route, escort, and time.

Chapter 6:

MEDICAL CARE

"Hemorrhage is the leading cause of preventable death on the battlefield."
- **DOD Joint Trauma System's *'Damage Control Resuscitation'***

Medical treatment, like war itself, has evolved through the ages. Advancements in technology and the development of new techniques has helped combatants stay alive after being injured. Preventing unnecessary deaths can be done through preventative medicine and treatment, as well as life support treatment if a patient was wounded in combat.

Throughout of the Global War on Terror, the United States and NATO learned how important rapid medical care was, especially following ambushes, roadside bombings, and during operations in rural areas where extraction was not immediately available. As stated above, hemorrhage, especially of the extremities, is the leading cause of preventable battlefield death, followed by tension pneumothorax (when, through a wound, air gets sucked through the chest wall and compresses the heart and lungs), and airway obstructions (blood, foreign objects, air pollutants, etc. blocking the airway). So, it became clear that the Department of Defense needed to begin researching and studying ways for ground forces to minimize these preventable deaths.

This journey to understand and implement truly effective in-field and pre-hospital care arguably began in the mid and late-1990s. It was in 2002 when the US Special Operations Command formed the Committee on Tactical Combat Casualty Care (CoTCCC). When the DoD began identifying casualty patterns and implementing new TCCC guidelines, preventable deaths began to decline. Today, combat and emergency medicine is more effective than ever before.

Tactical Combat Casualty Care is all about reducing preventable deaths and evacuating casualties from a combat zone. For much of the global war on terror, TCCC was used in conjunction with casualty evacuations (CASEVACs) and forward-deployed surgical teams and field hospitals. This system of rapid care was developed to aid, transport, and operate on trauma patients within "the golden hour." The golden hour of trauma care suggests than an injured party *must* get definitive trauma care within 60 minutes of the trauma to have the best chance of survival. TCCC is used to stabilize or secure the patient so that they can be evacuated to a location where definitive care can be provided.

TCCC is not only used in a military context, but also in any context where there is an injured party, such as during a mass shooting event. Therefore, TCCC is something that average civilians (not just soldiers or police) should learn in order to keep their fellow citizens alive.

TCCC and combat medicine are complex subjects that are beyond the scope of this document and the following information should not be considered sufficient study. A diligent student can extract the information presented and further their own knowledge through practice and professional, in-person instruction.

TCCC is broken up into 3 phases:

-   Care Under Fire (CUF)
-   Tactical Field Care (TFC)
-   Tactical Evacuation Care (TEC)

Each of these phases have different objectives that need to be accomplished.

1. CUF seeks to remove the patient from any direct threat and stabilize them as best as possible until more concentrated care can be delivered. Any heavy bleeding should be treated immediately. Then, once the immediate threat has subsided or the patient is as safe as possible from the threat, TFC begins.
2. TFC is about performing life support and treating immediate wounds. This stage is where, for example, a chest seal or splint may be applied. Bleeding should have

become controlled or stopped through various means. Physiological responses such as shock and hypothermia are also managed in this phase. TFC is all about treating immediate threats to the patient's life.

3. Finally, TEC is about evacuating the patient to so they can receive trauma support from dedicated medical professionals. At this stage, all wounds should be reassessed and monitored attentively. Airway management is performed to ensure the flow of oxygen and prevent any further damage to the brain or organs. If possible, medications are administered, such as painkillers, numbing agents, and antibiotics.

Those rendering aid should generally follow the acronym MARCH to determine what should be treated first.

Massive Hemorrhage – As stated previously, massive hemorrhage is the leading cause of preventable death. It should always be addressed first. Using tourniquets on limbs, packing junctions in the groin, neck, or armpit, and using seals on the torso and back can allow those rendering aid to stop the biggest threat to the patient's life and address other threats.

Airway – Airway patency should then be assessed. Any blockages or threats to the airway should be remediated. Securing the airway may be done with the use of an NPA (Nasopharyngeal Airway) or, if the airway threat is not critical or other care is necessary, the patient can be placed in the recovery position. Foreign bodies should be removed, if possible.

Respiration – The patient should be assessed for tension pneumothorax or other blast or penetrative trauma to the trunk of the patient. Any respiratory distress should be addressed. If tension pneumothorax is present, chest seals should be "burped," the patient should sit up (if awake) or be placed in the recovery position (if unconscious). If necessary, the chest may be decompressed with a needle/catheter unit (this should only be done by trained professionals or as a last-ditch effort, as proper needle placement is critical, and poor needle placement could cause further trauma to organs or arteries and lead to cardiac arrest or sudden death).

Circulation – A head-toe blood sweep should be performed with fresh gloves to assess for any previously unidentified wounds. Tourniquets and wound packings should be checked and re-applied or removed, if necessary. If bleeding is controlled and shock has not set in, tourniquets should be removed and replaced with pressure dressings within two hours of placement. In case of shock, saline or other resuscitation fluids should be administered, if available.

Hypothermia – Hypothermia is not only possible in cold environments. Through blood loss, the body loses heat and may enter a state of hypothermia. Wet clothes should be removed and replaced, if possible, with dry clothes. The patient should be removed from contact with wind or cold. Heat should be retained through the use of a hypothermia/space blanket.

All treatment should be documented and relayed to the trauma team that will be operating on the patient (if applicable), especially any administered medications. If analgesics are administered, this should also be relayed to prevent adverse reactions to other medications or accidental overdoses. It will help determine treatment plans and what other medications can be safely administered to help save the patient's life.

Prolonged field care is care provided outside of traditional care timelines (i.e., the golden hour), with the end goal being the delivery of the patient to definitive care. PFC is a poor situation to be placed in. Over the last two decades, U.S. and NATO forces have enjoyed rapid access to definitive care in the form of MEDEVACs and CASEVACs to trauma centers, field hospitals, or aid stations, often within 30-60 minutes. As the global war on terror fades away, and the western world once again turns their eyes and weapons towards the conventional armies of Russia, China, Iran, and North Korea, the ability to evacuate casualties will be actively challenged. To adapt to these future challenges in care, conventional forces, and especially special forces, have begun researching and implementing PFC into their systems of care.

PFC demands the successful implementation of ten capabilities:

1. *Monitor* – Providers should accurately monitor and document all patient vital signs
2. *Resuscitate* – Providers should effectively resuscitate patients, using fluids including whole blood if necessary
3. *Ventilate/Oxygenate* – Providers should provide positive pressure ventilation using bag valve masks or ventilators, if necessary
4. *Airway Management* – Providers should maintain airway patency to prevent aspiration or hypoxia

5. *Pain control/Sedation* – Providers should make use of appropriate pain relievers, as well as properly sedating any patients, if necessary, for any surgical procedures or to prevent further injury

6. *Physical Examination* – Providers should further assess their patient for any unaddressed injuries, including a full-body sweep with clean white or blue gloves and vital examination

7. *Ongoing Care* – Providers should keep the patient clean, warm, and dry. Clean air, food, and water should be provided. Wounds should be cared for. Further illnesses should be prevented

8. *Advanced Procedures* – Providers should execute any necessary or extreme interventions to the best of their ability with the intent of preserving life or preventing further injury that might threaten life

9. *Telemedicine* – Providers may establish communications with expert medical professionals (if security situation permits) who can provide guidance on specific procedures or tasks. Any communications should be established securely

10. *Prepare for Evacuation* – Providers should stage the patient to be transported to a setting that can provide definitive care. The patient should be secured and stabilized so as to prevent any further injury or threat to life

These ten capabilities will not completely remove the threat to a patient's life. Instead, they are intended to stabilize a patient who will likely not have access to definitive care within the golden hour.

When guerrillas are able to evacuate casualties, they need somewhere to take them for definitive care. Guerrillas can establish hidden clinics in austere environments. These clinics should be simplified, capable of being packed in and out by a few individuals in a relatively short period of time. The capabilities of these guerrilla clinics are still limited, but having a dedicated workspace to treat, triage, and operate on wounded individuals boost the capabilities of a guerrilla force.

These clinics would need to be far enough from any objectives, while remaining close enough to, or within, the area of operations to benefit any critically wounded individuals. Those transporting patients to the clinics should not always take a direct route unless otherwise necessary. In most cases, drivers and providers should utilize an Ambulance Exchange Point (AXPs). AXPs may be used to avoid detection or pursuit and to continue to conceal the location of the clinic, or to maintain a constant flow of casualties away from conflict and to definitive care in the event of a Mass Casualty Event. Potential locations for such clinics include abandoned or temporarily occupied residential or industrial sites, or underground locations. These locations likely have poor air circulation and may be filthy. Every effort should be made to effectively clean and sterilize all workspaces. All emissions from the clinic should be regulated; heat signature, radio emissions, electricity & internet usage, and verbal audio should all be closely monitored or mitigated so as the keep the clinic concealed.

Guerrilla clinics are extremely vulnerable. Higher tiered care providers, such as paramedics, health providers, and trauma surgery teams, are non-combatants when operating within their professional capacities. These clinics should not be seen as hardpoints. Accordingly, there is a risk that, if discovered, any individuals within the clinic will be detained, killed, interrogated, tortured, tried in tribunals and either imprisoned or executed, or any combination of the above. Every effort should be made to make clear the distinction between non-combatant healthcare providers and their patients from all combatant activities.

It is unlikely that guerrillas themselves will be able to fill the shoes of high-tier healthcare providers. Guerrilla forces will likely seek to recruit from sympathetic healthcare providers. Nevertheless, it is the guerrilla's job to wear multiple hats, and every opportunity should be taken to learn and expand operational skillsets so that one day, should the time come, the individual can respond to the best of their ability.

Disease is common during wartime, especially when spending prolonged periods of time in-field. For example, trench foot was extremely common in the World Wars and Vietnam. The condition stemmed from having wet feet for too long. It is a condition which, if left untreated, could lead to gangrene, amputations, and even death. Such as simple condition wrought havoc on even the most professional fighting forces.

Trench foot, and its impressive kill count, teaches us how important prevention is. If a fighting force can avoid contracting diseases or developing conditions, it can increase its effectiveness. If a fighter is forced to have his foot amputated because he could not be bothered to change his socks, then he becomes a detriment. If a fighter fails to purify or filter his drinking water and contracts cholera or giardia, he is no longer an asset and becomes a liability. Taking the steps necessary to prevent or treat disease is important for any fighting force, whether it is a conventional force or a guerrilla army. In any case, a loss of capability is something all warfighters should avoid, especially if it is easily preventable.

A common ailment is heat exhaustion. Heat exhaustion and heat stroke are serious concerns for any force, regardless of their composition. In the U.S., there are roughly 1,900 recorded deaths per year attributed to heat stroke and heat exhaustion. Both conditions are very common and need to be immediately treated. Symptoms include rapid pulse and excessive sweating. If someone develops heat exhaustion, their clothes should be loosened, they should be moved to a cool, shaded place, and given plenty of water. Raising the legs above the heart can be beneficial. Untreated heat exhaustion can lead to heat stroke, a condition where the core body temperature reaches at least 104°F, and includes symptoms such as agitation, slurred speech, and if left untreated, seizures, coma, and death. On the opposite side of temperature spectrum, hypothermia and frostbite are also very serious and should be immediately treated by getting dry and warm as soon as possible, with the goal of retaining body heat. All temperature related injuries should be given ample time to recover. Early recovery usually takes 24-48 hours, depending on the severity of the injury.

Other health issues that should be addressed stem from animals and parasites. Ticks, leeches, and mosquitos are common transmitters of diseases, some of which are difficult to treat and potentially fatal if left unchecked. Minimizing their impact on the overall force can be done by using unscented bug spray, washing regularly, performing routine hygiene checks, and medicating early (if possible/applicable). Ticks should be removed using tweezers or forceps, making sure to remove the head as well. Lyme disease and other ailments typically take 36+ hours to transmit, while other ailments can be transmitted much faster, so regular hygiene checks are important. Wearing pants and tucking them into the socks or boots can help keep ticks off the skin. Leeches may transmit bacterial infections, so it is important that they are removed quickly. Leeches should not be pulled directly off a patient, as parts of the jaw may remain and continue to pose a health risk. Salt, salt-water, or heat should be applied to the leech so that it falls off voluntarily. Any bleeding should be stopped with pressure, and the site should be thoroughly cleaned. Antibacterial ointment should be applied to the site and there should be regular checks for any infection. Mosquitos also transmit diseases and bites can either be simple annoyances or causes for concern. Any bites should be thoroughly cleaned, and a poultice of baking soda and water may be applied to reduce inflammation and itching, which may lead to infection. Similar steps to previous bites might be followed. Spider and snake bites can also hinder a force and can be life threatening. For non-venomous bites, infection is the biggest threat. Keeping the site clean, elevated, and regularly applying antibacterial ointment is normally more than enough. Additionally, most venomous spider bites are non-life threatening, only a small portion of them require any intense treatment, such as antivenom or tissue removal. Venomous snake bites are much more destructive to human tissue and often require professional intervention to treat. If a venomous snake bite occurs, individuals should seek antivenom treatment. Tourniquets should not be applied, nor should providers attempt to suck out any venom using their mouths or extractor pumps. The site of the bite should not be cleaned, as any residual venom on the skin could assist medical providers in administering proper antivenom. Too long without care, and snake bites can cause irreversible damage to tissue and nerves. If a hospital is too far away or cannot be reached within 6 hours, and the bite is on a limb, then the entire limb should be pressure wrapped and a splint should be applied. Efficient circulation should still be present in the limb, and circulation should be checked regularly.

Mentioned before, waterborne diseases can cripple any force. In fact, waterborne illnesses are among the leading causes of death worldwide. In the U.S. alone, waterborne diseases account for nearly 7,000 deaths in the U.S., or 3.4 million deaths globally. Most of the viruses, bacteria, and protozoa can be killed by boiling water for at least one minute or by using water filters capable of removing microbiological contaminants. Contracting waterborne illnesses can cause extreme dehydration through diarrhea and vomiting, high fevers, respiratory distress, body cramps, and in severe cases, seizures, shock, and death. Any of these symptoms alone could incapacitate a man. Therefore, it is critical that water be properly filtered and treated before being used for cleaning equipment or consumption. When in the field, any cleaning, bathing, or excretion should be done downstream from water collection points.

To summarize, take care of the feet, treat any ailments immediately and seriously, practice good hygiene always, and cook food and boil water thoroughly.

PSYCHOLOGICAL TRAUMA & STRESS MANAGEMENT

Most would agree that war is a necessary evil, and that it takes a certain breed of man or woman to endure it; a breed that may be born but also is created. A quote from Dave Grossman's book *"On Killing"* summarizes this position of studying the psychology of war and killing (without having killed, which most have not).

"We are truly, as one veteran put it to me, 'virgins studying sex,' but they can teach us what they have learned at such a dear price."

At the end of the day, the men fighting wars are human, whether they are guerrillas or conventionally trained. They have, generally, the same base psychology, the same brain chemicals as the rest of humanity. They enjoy the good things in life, and often seek them out in times of stress to cope with what they are experiencing; comfort, pleasure, brotherhood, purpose, escape.

Men go to war for a variety of reasons and the causes for war have not changed in the tens of thousands of years that humans have waged them. Anger, hatred, vengeance, freedom, survival, love, and loyalty have all been responsible for leading hundreds of millions of human beings to wage wars of extreme and often unspeakable violence against each other. These are strong motivations, and many warriors cling to them like a life raft while they drift through their conflict. They cling to their motivations because of the strong, primal emotions behind them and because they are also coping mechanisms. Having that purpose, that reason, or fuel, to continue fighting, is characteristic of any warfighter.

During the moments of lull in any conflict, there is time to reflect, whether there is a desire to reflect or not. And sometimes that reflection can be painful. Stretches of anxious boredom are not uncommon, and the subconscious mind may begin to ask questions that the conscious mind may not be ready, willing, or able to yet address. There are generally two ways for a warfighter to cope with what they are experiencing.

1. Keep the mind busy. Fill empty time with mental or physical work, tasks, or games that will prevent the mind from wandering and addressing questions or thoughts that it is unwilling or unable to address. This can be something as simple as playing a card game or working on completing important tasks that are meaningful to others or oneself. This method is not necessarily ideal as a long-term solution because the issue will more than likely not be resolved on its own and may become more unmanageable. As we have seen from the Global War on Terror, unmanaged trauma and stress can lead to crippling anxiety, depression, and, of course, suicide. Such catastrophic and senseless loss of life is unacceptable, both in times of war and peace.

2. Addressing the issue head-on. This method requires complete openness with oneself, the issue at hand, and a close confidant. It requires open discussion about what the person is experiencing (or has experienced) and how it is affecting them, as well as an understanding that the responses and emotions are natural. This method is used often to treat PTSD and focuses on shifting the perception of the experiences or emotions that the individual may be subject to. Honest journaling has also been found to help process traumatic experiences or loss. These are only small tools, but they are a point to start at. The goal is to process the traumatic experience and find a way to live with it.

Human psychology is a strange beast, but following the World Wars, the stigma surrounding the experiences of war began to fade away, and psychologists began developing methods to help soldiers cope with and overcome their experiences, both during and after. If one expects that they might one day fight for any reason, they should also understand how such an experience might affect them. Perhaps they can learn how to cope so they might be able to accomplish what they set out to do. It would be a tragedy for them to experience the horrors of war for no good reason.

Stress itself is a normal phenomenon, being broken up into two categories; Eustress & Distress. Eustress is a positive experience for the person. It is the difficulty or excited apprehension that leads to a rewarding experience. Examples of eustress are things like exercising, summiting a mountain, or having a child. Distress, however, is the problem. Distress occurs from losing a close friend or loved one, an injury, or a great loss. Distress can trigger physiological changes in the body, leading to things like depression, anxiety, hypertension, and other physical and mental health issues.

The best ways to work through extreme degrees of distress or trauma are often considered unmasculine or are associated with weakness or cowardice. However, the opposite is true, in that it takes an extremely strong and brave person to tackle an invisible enemy so that they may be at their best, both physically and mentally, to support their brothers and sisters against a physical enemy. Examples of stress management include:

1. *Talk* – Discuss the situation with trusted people. Encourage a culture of openness and honesty from others (within OPSEC parameters)
2. *Write* – Write about the problem with openness and honesty. Expect that no one else will read the words unless you choose to share them
3. *Address Physical Responses* – Physical signs of stress or anxiety include constantly elevated shoulders, obsessive/compulsive tapping feet or feet raised onto the ball of the foot, rapid breathing or heartrate, trembling, an impending sense of doom, excessive or unexplained sweating, or muscular weakness. Combat these symptoms by breathing deeply, making and releasing a fist, and

intentionally relaxing the muscles. Focusing on what can be controlled, rather than what cannot, is also beneficial

4. *Avoid Substances* – Substance abuse can become a very real problem, especially when it is used to escape or minimize the effects of stress. Alcohol, tobacco, and drugs prevent individuals from being at their best and therefore threaten the individual, the group, and the mission, and should be avoided at all costs. Substance abuse is like putting a band aid on a malignant tumor. Suppressing the symptoms will not solve the issue at hand.

Chapter 7:

COMMUNICATIONS

"We are all now connected by the Internet, like neurons in a giant brain."
- **Stephen Hawking**

While Chapter 4 discussed how guerrilla forces should communicate with the general public and the enemy, this chapter will focus on how they can communicate with each other. Signals Intelligence works both ways, and Unconventional Groups will always be at a disadvantage as it is impossible for them to have even a fraction of the infrastructure that a state-sponsored unit has. Therefore, guerrilla forces have to make up for the lack of infrastructure and funding with clever and unconventional solutions to their communications problems.

While radio is still the primary communication method that forces use in-field, Internet and intranet usage is being integrated, especially in countries that have better communications and internet infrastructure. A good example of internet being used to communicate would be how ISIS social media coordinators would communicate securely with their supporters in western countries, such as France. It was through the use of the internet messaging, social media monitoring, and other unencrypted communication platforms that a cell was able to coordinate a highly sophisticated attack on Paris from Brussels in 2015. Despite some of the perpetrators being on terrorism watchlists, they were still able to acquire firearms and the tools necessary for homemade explosives. While all the attackers and organizers were eventually captured, killed, or committed suicide attacks, this attack highlighted how easy it was for groups to communicate and coordinate, even across international borders. The attack also reinforced the mentality that state intelligence agencies have towards internet privacy.

Radio was adopted by conventional forces because it relayed critical information exponentially faster than relying on carrier pigeons or message runners. It also enabled the secure transmission of messages without requiring the traditional ciphers that were so common before the first World War. Early radios were extremely heavy and rudimentary and were not sufficient for any practical use. It was not until WWII where radio finally became an incredible asset and where radios first became man portable.

Today, many seemingly mundane things depend on radio waves, including mobile phones and garage door openers. However, some extremely important tools also utilize radio waves, such as cell towers, GPS receivers, radar systems, and aircraft. Radio waves are all around us, and everyday people can use readily available tools to broadcast their own communications, but also to patch in and listen to (or interfere with) the radio waves others are emitting.

Radio waves are just a piece of what is called the electromagnetic spectrum. The spectrum is made up of a variety of different frequencies, with the lower frequencies having longer wavelengths and the stronger frequencies having shorter wavelengths. Imagine electromagnetic waves as if they are the waves in a pond. Throwing a small rock into the pond will create small waves with short distances between each wave. Throwing a larger rock will create larger waves with more distance between them. The distance, or wavelength, between each resulting wave is indicative of the frequency of the wave. The longer the wave, the lower the frequency. The shorter the wave, the higher the frequency. Radio waves are the longest waves on the electromagnetic spectrum. The wave itself is just the changing, or reciprocating energies in the electric and magnetic fields. As electric currents are introduced,

Radio frequencies can be emitted by introducing electric ener to transmitters. Radios themselves function by sending and receiving these electromagnetic waves. Within the radio waves, there are also sine waves, and sine waves contain the information that we hear through speakers or see on electronic displays. Think of sine waves as a written letter, and the radio waves as the mailman carrying the letter from one mailbox to another. Each radio has three primary parts; the transmitter, the antenna, and the receiver. The transmitter generates the radio waves by introducing bursts of electricity to disrupt the magnetic field and it gathers the data, the antenna propels the wave outward, and the receiver captures the waves and translates the information into a digestible medium.

When the 21st century began, few could have predicted the impact that the internet would have on society. Aspects of the internet were already becoming common, like online marketplaces and social media platforms, but it took time for humanity to weaponize it. Today, the internet is used to reach millions of people in a very short amount of time, and the speed at which information is accessed has made disinformation campaigns effective tools for state powers, namely the United States and Russia.

The internet has also served The People. The open internet has become a marketplace for learning but also for secure communicating. Tools such as Signal, Keybase, and Telegram offer end-to-end encryption, which is a powerful form of encryption but, like everything, has its weaknesses. There are also tools such as Tor (The Onion Browser), which is used to, ideally, provide anonymity while accessing the internet. Tor should always be used in conjunction with a VPN. There are also operating systems that allow you to access the internet while also ensuring nothing you say or do is saved to your device, such as TailsOS, which uses Tor to access the internet and "forgets" the data that would normally be saved under another OS, like Windows. Devices can also be outfitted with software that will completely wipe all information on a devices hard drive, such as DBAN (Darik's Boot and Nuke). These types of programs can be booted from storage devices such as USBs if the owner believes that the device may be seized. Journalists operating in less-than permissive environments have used DBAN and similar programs in the past. Email has also seen an increase in privacy, with services such as ProtonMail offering encrypted email.

Communicating via internet always poses a threat to those communicating. Encryption can be cracked and spoofed IP addresses can be traced. It is important that when communicating via the internet those communicating should not always be overt in their statements or intentions.

Using these tools (and the many others that are available) in conjunction with each other, changing passwords frequently and never using the same one twice, and using operational security while communicating can keep identities and intentions hidden from anyone who would seek to intercept private communications.

SIGNALS

Sometimes, using technology to communicate is less than ideal. Some forces have found ways to alert each other to specific information and threats by using visual signals and sounds. For example, in small unit tactics, hand signals or specific weapon manipulations (such as "halo-ing" with white light in CQB) can be used to quickly communicate information that cannot or should not be verbally shared. Other examples of forces using signals instead of electronic communications would be the use of visual cues such as burning tires (or other petroleum-based items that produce thick, black signal smoke), flares, flashlights, and lasers. Examples of audible cues include bird calls, horns, gunshots, and whistles.

As technology advances and even the most rudimentary insurgency force is gaining access to communication technology, state forces have stepped up their abilities to detect and track radio signals, especially with the rapid proliferation of drones. Sometimes, it is better to use physical signals to communicate on a local level than to send radio signals out into the ether. This practice of intentionally reducing signal emissions to an absolute minimum is becoming doctrine even for conventional forces.

Sometimes all sources of communication are being monitored, or they are simply too risky to use at any moment. It is at these times that communication must be done surreptitiously. There are several ways to conduct this type of communication, and there are examples of it during wartime, military occupation, and times of heightened, but still cold, geopolitical tension (such as during the Cold War).

One example would be number stations, which have seen extensive use. In the United States alone, numerous people in defense and intelligence agencies have been caught and tried for communicating with foreign powers, such as the Soviet Union and Cuba, through coded radio messages. These stations can use a combination of words or numbers that are seemingly nonsensical, and often are. The covert communication should not sound strange or on-the-nose, as it would attract unwanted attention to the specific word or phrase. Number stations and code stations have been used since World War 1 and can be disguised as a normal radio station or be overtly dedicated to delivering instructions to a cell by spamming useless information while the intended recipient has the key to decipher the seemingly useless information.

Arguably the most common form of covert communication is the use of dead drops. A dead drop is a physical drop location where an agent or a handler can plant money, information, or documents to be picked up a later time. Dead drops can be are hidden in an unsuspecting location, often in public. Dead drops can also be delivered wirelessly, similar in function to Apple's AirDrop feature. The downside of dead drops is that if anyone who knows the location of the dead drop is caught and interrogated, they may give up the location. State intelligence services may then either capture the other participant when they go to retrieve the dead drop, or, more likely, begin feeding false information to the recipient.

PACE is a framework designed to assist mission planners to lay out their methods of communication from most secure and available to the most unsecure and extreme. PACE is an acronym standing for Primary, Alternate, Contingency, and Emergency. Typically, the primary form of communication will be a form of secure radio. As communication methods become compromised, the PACE plan allows decision makers to continue to execute their mission and maintain communications with team members or off-site leadership. Cellular and Satellite phones are extremely unsecure and should only be used as a contingency or emergency form of communicating. Even using visual or auditory signals, if electronic communication becomes entirely useless or dangerous, can be effective in communicating information.

Chapter 8:

CIVIL AFFAIRS

"Politics is war without bloodshed…"

- **Mao Zedong**

As discussed in Chapter 4, the overall goal of any successful insurgency should be the find a way to gain the Hearts & Minds of The People. Without the support of the general population, not much (in terms of long-term social or political change) can be done. With a strong enough militant force, territory can be taken, and enemies can be defeated, but if the people hate the insurgents, any and all gains will be temporary. So, along with effective propaganda efforts, successful insurgencies should look to work with the people and offer aid whenever possible.

So, what *is* Civil Affairs and how could it be implemented by an insurgency?

Civil Affairs, at its core, is about understanding, engaging with, and influencing the civilian population within the theater of conflict. Any force, whether it is a burgeoning insurgency or an established conventional army, must capture the support of the people, or, at the very least, strive to understand the population as much as possible. Understanding the population, its culture, and its social psychology has been mentioned in this work before, but the understanding of the population is derived from effective civil reconnaissance and civil affairs operations.

This brings us to the question; how is it implemented? Civil Affairs operations include civil engagement, or directly engaging with the populace, the purpose of which is to foster cohesive, positive relationships with the locals and reduce the influence an adversary may have on them. Examples include:

- Conducting food and water distribution programs
- Rebuilding or paying for property that may have been destroyed or damaged in fighting or accidents, regardless of fault
- Playing games with local kids
- Planting community gardens and teaching other valuable skills
- Promoting information sharing and transparency (while maintaining OPSEC/PERSEC)
- Serving whenever possible

Another point that needs to be addressed with civil affairs is the political tension that naturally occurs during an asymmetric conflict. As the nonincumbent political force attempts to take control, the force needs to have relations with the local population, an ambassadorship of sorts. Without representatives who understand both the strategic objectives of the allied force but also the social and political concerns that the population has, there is unlikely to be any constructive gains between the population and the force.

Consider the first days of the wars in Iraq and Afghanistan. Quite early on, the Americans used translators and cultural attaches to help soldiers, especially special forces, verbally understand the natives. However, it took some time for the conventional military to adapt to the cultural sensitivities that the locals had and to understand what the locals wanted. Much of the communication went through local elders and hired or volunteer interpreters. Many of the early operations within Iraq were simply rebuilding much of the infrastructure that had been destroyed in the invasion, including water systems and canals, hospitals, and TV stations. When strikes hit these locations, it naturally created animosity for the American forces, which took a significant amount of time and effort (mostly by Civil Affairs teams, known as CATs) to fix.

Specifically with Afghanistan, CATs featured heavily, as political stability was the overall goal of American operations. CATs would be inserted into small villages as well as provincial capitals to conduct outreach with local leaders as well as provide humanitarian relief, such as deliveries of food or blankets. By providing services and meeting with local political and religious leaders, the CATs were able to begin soliciting support for their mission. The CATs handled themselves differently from the normal soldiers that the local leaders had already met; they seemed to share concern for the people and showed an interest in supporting the local population through projects that would increase their standards of living. It was these relationships that then enabled an atmosphere of cooperation, which eventually led to special forces teams being deployed to strike targets identified by locals. It was not just morality and love and friendship, however. In many cases, locals had to be bribed with cash or intimidated into cooperation. These methods can easily backfire, so they should be used as last resorts. This method of using CATs was a part of the Clear-and-Hold counterinsurgency strategy that we will return to later.

At the end of the day, Civil Affairs is about interacting with the locals (especially political, social, and religious leaders) and finding middle ground that will create a symbiotic environment in which both sides get what they want. Providing selfless services (that is, actually caring about the impact the service will have), bridging gaps (whether they be social, religious, or linguistic), and developing meaningful relationships with people will help garner support from the local forces. These are methods that can be used by both the insurgent and the counterinsurgent, implementation is the only difference. Counterinsurgents would be better suited to building hospitals or running education drives, while insurgents might be more inclined to focusing on the relationships, small acts of kindness and selflessness, and appealing to the moral, political, or religious tendencies of a populace. It is civil affairs that will pave the way for a peaceful transition from military conflict to a civilian-led government. Successful civil affairs operations will yield resources, intelligence, and moral victories for the insurgent force, which are all critical to long-term success.

Civil affairs operations have three major functions:

1. Civil Reconnaissance
2. Civil Engagement
3. Civil Information Management

Discussed briefly in Chapter 5, civil reconnaissance is the deliberate collection, analysis, and dissemination of intelligence gathered on civil features. Such intelligence can include profile packets on buildings and structures, individuals, organizations, and events, as well as intangible features such as the economy of an area, its history, language, and cultural norms. Civil reconnaissance should be an ongoing pursuit and should also be consistently reviewed. Any changes to the civil space may be important to key decisionmakers. Information should be cross-referenced, and new sources should be developed regularly. Civil reconnaissance also assesses the impact that the insurgents and nonincumbent political force are having on the population. This information can allow leadership to adjust course, if necessary.

Civil engagement (CE) is the focused and targeted tactical mission that generates intelligence during civil reconnaissance operations. CE missions seek to accomplish several objectives:

- Mitigate the impact of military operations on the civilian populace

- Mitigate the impact of civilian activities on military operations

- Develop symbiotic ties between friendly forces and civilian entities

- Pave the way for a civilian-led transitional government

- Mediate conflicts between the insurgent force and civilians

- Facilitate intelligence collection and information dissemination

CE is intended to create close ties with the civilian population. This allows for more effective dissemination of propaganda, more reliable and frequent intelligence, and more cooperation from locals. A strategic goal for any insurgent force's CE missions would be to become integral to civil society, in a way that the society could not function in its current form without the presence, cooperation, and support of the insurgent force and its political arm. By doing so, the CE missions would supplant the incumbent military and government entities.

Those engaging in CE missions should be intellectually mature. They should be natural negotiators and have an interest in understanding opposing viewpoints in an honest way while also understanding how their own biases could impact their understanding. CE missions are intended to develop relationships and relationships cannot be built without nuance, sensitivity, and mutual understanding.

Civil Information Management (CIM) is the process of gathering, analyzing, and disseminating information gathered from local informants and civilians in the operating area. The CIM process follows several steps:

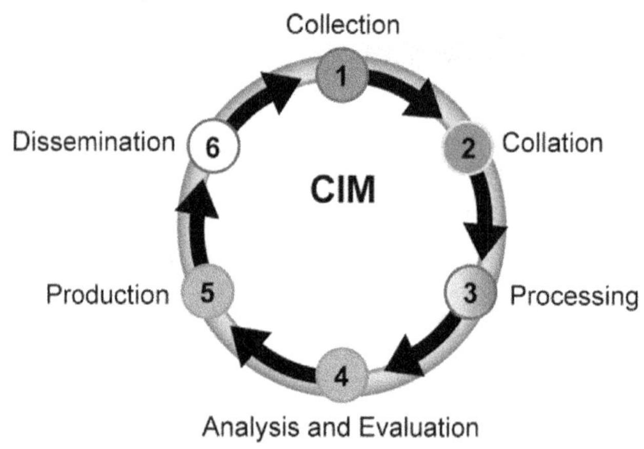

Step 1: Collection

Collection of raw information is the first step in the CIM process. This can be done via *Key Leader Engagements* (KLEs), such as what has been with seen with tribal leaders in Iraq and Afghanistan, as well as through Civil Action Programs (CAPs). These are targeted engagements with locals that are done to illicit support and intelligence from the locals, but also in a genuine effort to improve their lives, their communities, and develop long lasting relationships rooted in trust.

KLEs are initiated by finding key leaders within the community who may be open to dialogue or are sympathetic to the cause. These leaders should be key decisionmakers or influencers in the social, economic, or political spheres or a community or region. These leaders should have sufficient capability to influence on behalf of friendly interests, and such capability should be assessed before the KLE is initiated.

The KLE should be prepared for by including relevant members on the team and by rehearsing the meeting. During the meet, the engagement leader should directly address the leader and steer the conversation always toward the objective, never getting distracted by issues that could detract from the objective or cause excessive offense. The engagement leader should take ownership of past mistakes and for future promises. Always execute KLEs with honesty and show genuine interest in the target leaders concerns. Once a relationship is established, it should be maintained and strengthened through mutual aid.

Civil Action Programs are operations that are undergone to support the local population and undermine the financially superior methods of a conventional force. A conventional force will have significantly more financial capital and will be able to pursue more numerous and robust CAPs, such as improving infrastructure, reinforcing food security, or supporting economic development. Oftentimes, however, conventional forces seek to "throw money" at the local population rather than address their needs in a holistic way. Unconventional groups should recognize that they are at a disadvantage in this regard and should strive in every way to approach relations with the local population from a place of genuine care, something that conventional forces often lack.

Unconventional groups should begin by assessing what needs a community has. Such needs can be discovered through the initial civil reconnaissance framework, from discussing needs directly with citizens, or through KLEs. Once the needs are known, they can be addressed.

Issues that can be addressed and solved through CAP projects include things such as:

- Fixing damaged property from fighting or other operations
- Planting and maintaining community gardens
- Volunteering at food banks, fairs, festivals, markets, shelters, etc.
- Protecting culturally important landmarks

Any issue that is important to the local community can become the subject of a CAP project, resource permitting. Supporting the local population is the key to garnering support and building a strong, resilient, and independent community. By completing and participating in such projects, an unconventional group can forge ties with the locals, bringing in reliable and more frequent intelligence.

Of course, due to the public-facing nature of civil affairs work, team members should always be alert and should be very intentional in their actions. They should always be professional and should not participate in any overtly "criminal" activity.

The information gained from these activities should ultimately assist friendly forces in their pursuit of engaging the enemy and/or supporting the local community. Anything else is useless.

Step 2: Collation

Each bit of information that is collected by the civil affairs team is a piece of the puzzle. Collation is the step in the process in which intelligence gathered during KLEs, CAPs, and other intelligence gathering missions is assembled and organized into categories in preparation for the next steps in the CIM cycle.

Intelligence should be organized in such a way that enables thorough processing and eases analysis. Relevant intelligence should be secure but accessible, so that the civil affairs team and intelligence analysts are able to sift through what is relevant and what is not. Information regarding individuals, for example, should not be included with information regarding a location unless there is a relevant correlation.

Step 3: Processing

The information collected through KLEs, CAPs, and other intelligence gathering operations is considered "raw" data. It is in this step that analysts will begin to parse through the vast amounts of raw data to obtain information that is relevant to the current tactical or strategic objectives.

Raw information, such as traffic or patrol patterns, natural hazards, etcetera, can be compiled into reports to ascertain more information. Certain bits of raw data may support a micro-view of the situation and make it difficult to view how that information fits into the big picture. It is important to take a step back and assess how the information is relevant and how it can be applied. The opposite is true as well. It is possible to become too focused on the big picture or the strategic goal(s) and miss seemingly minor pieces of the puzzle.

Information gained may not be relevant in the moment but may become critical in the future. Therefore, processing the raw data into an organized system is critical to long term success. Excel sheets, google documents, and other data processing programs can be used for processing, but it needs to be stressed that keeping information secure is paramount. Poor handling of raw or processed data can aid the opposition.

Step 4: Analysis & Evaluation

In this step, it is the job of the analyst to sort through the compiled and organized data to identify patterns, behavior, or opportunities. By identifying these things, the analyst is able to piece together bits of data to create a whole. This "whole" can give analysts, decision makers, and fighters the ability to clearly see what is impacting their ability to operate within the area and provide a variety of options with which they can proceed.

To analyze the data that has been processed, the analyst must have the ability to think critically. Critical thinking is a tool that allows the analyst to detach and utilize reason and fact, rather than opinion and assumption. It is equally important to recognize internal biases and make a cognitive effort to avoid assumptions, as these processes are rarely, if ever, rooted in truth or fact. Adhering to these standards, the analyst is then able to form a hypothesis with the information they find. This hypothesis should be tested using available information and deductive reasoning. By understanding trends, patterns, information gleaned from ASCOPE analyses, and the SOPs or ROEs of the opposition, the analyst can come to a reasonable conclusion that can then be shared with colleagues and decisionmakers.

The analyst should be open to collaboration with other analysts, as well as subject matter experts and individuals with firsthand experience of the situation on the ground. This will enable to analyst to identify their biases or assumptions more easily, as well as get the valuable insight that others with different experiences have.

Step 5: Production

In Production, analysts transform the data they have analyzed into digestible products than can act as vehicles for that information. Examples of such products include:

- Maps
- Photographs and other digital media
- Written and verbal reports
- Briefings for decision makers

Each product should be accompanied by supporting data, so that any questions or concerns that may arise when reviewing the product(s) may be appropriately answered or addressed. Products should be easily digestible, understandable, and concise. This step is relatively straightforward and is largely administrative. As always, any products derived from gathered data and intelligence should be kept secure.

Step 6: Dissemination

Finally, dissemination is when information is passed on to leadership and team members on a relevant basis. Disseminating the produced intelligence allows for decision makers to remain informed and up to date on current activities, patterns, and opportunities regarding friendly forces, hostile combatants, and the civilian population. Properly disseminating produced intelligence facilitates action.

Dissemination can be done through several direct and indirect channels. This should be done at the discretion of the analysts. Compartmentalization and information security are key, both to keep produced intelligence out of the hands of hostile elements, but also to keep friendly forces from being exposed to sensitive information. This removes the opportunity for disillusioned friendly forces to share information that should be kept secure, either intentionally or unintentionally.

It has been said numerous times throughout this work, but without the support of The People, little in the way of long-term change will be gained. Civil affairs is the direct cooperation between friendly forces and the civilian population, and such activities should be of the utmost importance to any unconventional group.

It is important to note that Civil Affairs should not be conducted for its own sake. A true guerrilla force that seeks freedom and security for its people should conduct Civil Affairs out of an authentic sense of charity, love, and fellowship, not simply to garner support.

Chapter 10:

GUERRILLA WARFARE

"The guerrilla fights the war of the flea, and his military enemy suffers the dog's disadvantage: too much to defend; too small, ubiquitous, and agile an enemy to come to grips with."

- **Robert Taber**

Even with the most cursory online search, the average man could become a guerrilla with sufficient know-how with just a few days. Guerrilla warfare is the last resort when the State no longer enables the People to live peaceful, prosperous lives, and when the State makes it impossible to enable social or political change through peaceful, "legal" methods. When the State begins using violence and intimidation to suppress the natural rights of the People, it is only logical that they will resort to the only remaining viable source of change: Guerrilla Warfare.

After all, The Committee of Five who wrote the American Declaration of Independence declared the natural right of revolution, which was unanimously adopted by the First Continental Congress of The United States:

"We hold these truths to be self-evident, that all men are created equal, that they are endowed by their Creator with certain unalienable Rights, that among these are Life, Liberty and the pursuit of Happiness -- That to secure these rights, Governments are instituted among Men, deriving their just powers from the consent of the governed, -- <u>That whenever any Form of Government becomes destructive of these ends, it is the Right of the People to alter or to abolish it, and to institute new Government, laying its foundation on such principles and organizing its powers in such form, as to them shall seem most likely to effect their Safety and Happiness.</u>"

Guerrilla Warfare itself has been the subject of countless works, and there have been far better sources than this one that have delved into the subject. Guerrillas themselves have documented their experiences, Generals have studied the method and reported their findings, and we can open any history book written about the 20th century and it will be inundated with tales of guerrillas waging war against governments. Because of this, it would be irresponsible to create even more literature on the matter. Instead, this chapter will address some tactics, but mostly strategic thinking and concepts that could assist fighters in implementing the tactics, leading others, and succeeding long-term.

GUERRILLA STRATEGIES & STRATEGIC OBJECTIVES

When thinking about guerrilla warfare, most people forget that it is a distinctly strategic practice, and they fall into the trap of focusing too heavily on the tactical implementation. Guerrilla warfare is successfully implemented with long-term goals in mind, and not by simply winning the next engagement. That mindset (thinking ahead only to the next gunfight or ambush) is what causes guerrilla fighters to fail. They are unable to see the "big picture" of why they are fighting or how they will achieve their goal, and they begin to succumb to attrition or fatigue.

Long term, the goal of the guerrilla fighter is to assert independence from a centralized foe, usually an incumbent government or invading military. They are either seeking to overthrow the government authority and continue to govern the same country (revolution) or to form a new government with a new governing model within a particular area after deposing the threat (secession). Mao Zedong, while opposing the powerful US-backed Chiang Kai-shek Chinese Nationalist government, developed a 3-phase strategy to raise the guerrilla force into a powerful military and political body that can directly oppose the central authority.

Phase 1: Organization

Phase 1 focuses on establishing both the literal and figurative *base* of the guerrilla force. The guerrilla force slowly (and quietly) begins organizing its forces, establishing its political authority in local governments, and developing relationships with locals (politicians, food producers, etc.). This phase is usually undertaken in rural and geographically difficult areas. It is important that the force keeps a low profile during this stage, sending out highly motivated and intelligent members to develop the necessary social/political ties as well as to recruit members. All the while, continuing the teambuilding for the force itself, creating a tightly knit and dedicated force with a strong communal identity.

Phase 2: Insurrection and Expansion

It is in Phase 2 that direct clashes begin between the guerrilla forces and the centralized government or military. Phase 2 is the longest of the 3 Phases. Teams or companies will be sent out to various areas to conduct operations to engage and destabilize the existing government or military force. These include the ambushes and raids that guerrillas are well-known for. Other activities include propaganda dissemination, community outreach (civil affairs), and assassination of high-level individuals. Fighters actively avoid direct, pitched confrontation with conventional forces, opting instead for hit-and-run tactics and engagements that are initiated and ended on their own terms. Phase 2 could also be called the "logistics" phase, as it is imperative that the guerrilla force begins acquiring supplies and arms to support its transition into a more conventional force. Arms collection is a primary goal during Phase 2. All activities conducted in Phase 1 continue during Phase 2.

Phase 3: Decision or Defeat

It is in this phase in which the guerrilla force should begin to resemble a conventional force. Phase 3 is where the centralized foe is finally defeated and overthrown. Traditional military tactics and strategies begin to be used in conjunction with the traditional guerrilla raids and ambushes. Phase 3 is about militarily destroying the enemy. At this point, the hearts of the People should be with the guerrilla force and the centralized force should have little, if any, political or social influence. All activities conducted in Phases 1 and 2 continue during Phase 3.

Mao's 3-Phase model is broad enough, but also not too specific, that it can be used effectively in just about any context. Not only was it coined and successfully used by Mao himself in China, but Vo Nguyen Giap and Ho Chi Minh of Vietnam effectively used this model to develop their forces against the French and the Americans. Fidel Castro and Che Guevara also used a rough outline of this method, and it helped establish their control in Cuba. It is noteworthy that the most successful guerillas of the 20th century all used this 3-Phase method.

Castro's early failures could have been because he focused too heavily on the tactical aspect of guerrilla warfare. He returned to Cuba after his initial failure to overthrow the Batista government and his subsequent exile. Following Phase 1 of Mao's strategy, he would set up his base in the dense forests and rough mountains of the Sierra Maestra range. From here, they sought out recruits from the nearby farms and cities. Then followed Phase 2, with bombings, ambushes, and raids against the established Batista regime across the island. They eventually pushed the military out of the Sierra Maestra region entirely and established complete control. When the Batista regime returned with force, including air power, Castro's guerrillas were so effective in their use of defensive fortifications, ambushes, and counterattacks, combined with the Batista regime's poor military leadership, that hundreds defected from the Cuban army to join Castro. Thus, beginning Phase 3. The guerrillas began to resemble a conventional army, conducting direct strikes against what remained of the Army surrounding the Sierra Maestra mountains. Soon, Castro's influence could be found in even the highest ranks of the Cuban military.

Even the American Continental Army loosely followed his model, beginning with the minutemen from Lexington and Concord counterattacking the British and surrounding Boston (Phase 1), being then formed into a loose conventional force led by George Washington but still conducting guerrilla warfare (Phase 2), and then, finally, being trained by the Prussian Officer Baron von Steuben into a professional force that could directly face British forces (Phase 3). When the war began to close, American regulars were a force to be reckoned with and the remaining militias and guerrillas began to flock to the Continental army for status and commissions.

Almost all successful insurgencies grow to become conventional forces in some form, as history has shown. Those that refuse to embrace that evolution are the ones that die in their infancy, unable to accomplish anything other than useless bloodshed. Those that are fighting for ideals, such as Liberty, or to overthrow a tyrannical force, should seek to implement Mao's model in some degree. Its breadth allows room for the guerrilla force to adapt the 3-Phase model to their specific circumstances, but its specificity provides a literal step by step guide that the force can use to help guide their short- and long-term decision making with clear goals.

Again, guerrilla warfare, and especially the associated tactics, have been written about at great length by much more knowledgeable writers. This section will serve to simply underscore some of the more common and effective tactics that guerrillas may, and often do, use in combat against conventional foes.

The Ambush

The Ambush is the bread and butter of a guerrilla force. Conventional forces are typically loud and sluggish, and with a good intelligence apparatus, the guerrilla force can determine where and when an enemy patrol or convoy might pass by. At its most basic level, an ambush is the use of surprise and violence of action to engage an enemy force with the goal of destroying them, harassing them, delaying them, or capturing them or their supplies. Ambushes are deeply connected to the landscape, and detail how good terrain reconnaissance can be used.

When conducting an ambush, there are 2 distinct elements: The Assault Element and the Security Element(s)

- The *Assault Element* is the group responsible for directly engaging the enemy within a predefined kill zone. It is the Assault Element that conducts a majority of the ambush itself. The Assault Element also assaults the kill zone following the ambush in order to capture any supplies of personnel.

- The *Security Element(s)* are responsible for providing security for the Assault Element. They may be placed behind the Assault Element or along the flanks to observe for enemy reinforcements or counter ambush elements. Security Elements may also be used to prevent the hostile force from escaping the kill zone. The number of Security Elements is determined by personnel availability and terrain considerations.

Ambushes are generally divided into 3 classifiers: Category, Formation, and Type.

- **Category** is used to define the speed and organization for the ambush itself. An ambush can be *hasty* (thrown together with limited information or preparation based on visual contact with an incoming enemy force) or *deliberate* (organized long before a specific target arrives and has established security and blocking elements prepared)
- **Formation** is used to define the shape of the ambush. There are generally 3 formations that are used, although there can be variations based on context and resource availability. The 3 formations are *Linear* (where the entire assault force is aligned along a natural boundary and is an equal distance from the kill zone), *L-Shaped* (in which a small leg of the ambush force is placed along the flank or rear of the target), and *V-Shaped* (where there are assault elements on both sides of an opposing force and where the assault elements grow closer to the opposing force the further they draw into the kill zone)
- **Type** is used to define the scope of the ambush. There are 2 relevant types of ambushes, *Point* (where a specific location is targeted to inflict the most possible damage against an incoming force) and *Area* (where a large area is selected to encompass multiple point ambushes, usually against a numerous foe that can be funneled through multiple kill zones).

Ambushes follow the same basic rules across conflicts; however, belligerents may alter or add to the ambush based on their own regional contexts. For example, the Viet Cong used tree cover to prevent responsive American air support. The Viet Cong also used trees to plant machine gun nests and snipers. The Finnish used *Motti* ambushes during the Soviet-Finnish wars, in which they would use ski warfare to divide large convoys or sections of troops into individual and manageable pockets. The Afghan Mujahideen would use horses to descend upon Soviet convoys from the mountain slopes. Mexican cartels conduct mobile ambushes using vehicles, in which they roll up on a static target (i.e., guards at a gas station or a target vehicle stuck in traffic), dismount, engage, and then exfil from the area just as fast as they arrived.

Ambushes are fluid and open to change. Terrain, intelligence, available weaponry & equipment, and manpower are all factors that should be addressed when planning an deliberate ambush. A guerilla force should bear in mind, however, that the same information is available to the opposing force, and they can successfully anticipate ambushes that are in predicable locations.

Use of Terrain

Guerrillas are masters of using terrain to their advantage. Guerrillas should operate out of difficult terrain that conventional forces would struggle to access. What makes conventional forces so powerful is their use of combined arms. Most, if not all historically successful guerrilla groups have used difficult terrain to increase their mobility, prevent or diminish retaliatory operations, and evade detection. Francis Marion used the swamps of South Carolina to slow down and restrict the pursuing British cavalry who normally dominated the plains, hills, and fields. Al-Qaeda and the Taliban used the foreboding Hindu Kush Mountain range to make themselves difficult to reach and to develop avenues of escape into Pakistan. It was in these same mountains that the Afghans would successfully resist, over countless generations, several empires that were numerically and technologically superior. Guerrillas who operate out of flat areas (such as much of Iraq or the heartlands of the United States) do not have much access to difficult terrain, and so conventional forces have much less difficulty finding and engaging fighters. It is in these areas that urban fighting typically occurs the most.

Efficient use of terrain can allow an insurgent force to establish strongholds, usually in towns or villages. The use of strongholds by guerrillas is rarely a winning tactic, yet they can be very difficult to take. The Dagestani Murids fortified themselves in the village of Gimry in 1832 and inflicted heavy casualties against the Russian forces before being overrun. During the Battle of Takur Ghar in Afghanistan. Al-Qaeda forces, using machine gun nests and bunkers concealed in the heavy snow and the rugged terrain at the top of the mountain, were able to inflict heavy damage against the American special forces that sought to dislodge them. The Jewish Sicarii managed to hold out for 3 years against the Romans at Masada due to its extreme geography.

The Sicarii did not fight, however, instead opting to kill themselves due to the hopelessness of their situation. Had they decided to fight, they would have surely still lost, but their terrain advantage would have likely enabled them to do significant damage to the incoming Roman Legions. Guerrillas can temporarily hold positions but should always opt to "melt" away and disappear before conventional forces have the chance to bear down on them using combined arms or massive forces. Should the guerrilla force seek to hold a location, they should employ all tools available to prevent being overrun. Defensive operations will be discussed in a later section.

Terrain is a major asset for guerrillas, and is calculated into considerations for most, if not all, tactical and strategic decisions, such as where to prepare an ambush or what checkpoints can be raided. Efficient use of terrain is a critical factor for unconventional forces.

Raids

Raids, like ambushes, are extremely important for guerrilla forces to conduct. They can be used to resupply arms and ammunition, destroy critical enemy equipment, to push out enemy forces from a particular area, to gather intelligence, or to simply attack an easy target for a morale boost. Raids can also be used to target specific objectives developed from intelligence, such as a high-profile individual or an observation post, but also to distract reactionary forces, such as aircraft or quick reaction forces, while another objective is secured that would normally have been under heavier protection.

Raids should be conducted quickly and with a strong emphasis on violence of action. The guerrilla force should insert into the area and establish themselves at an ORP (objective rally point). Using speed and surprise, they then leave the ORP for the objective and overwhelm the defending force as quickly as possible, using all available weapons and resources to shock the defenders. Since guerrillas usually oppose powerful conventional militaries, the risk of enemy aircraft, armor, or quick reaction forces being deployed to help defend the site and repel the attackers is high. So, to prevent being overwhelmed themselves, the guerrilla forces should seek to get in and out of the area as quickly as possible. If gains are not made early on, the guerrilla force should elect to cut their losses, return to the ORP, and exfil.

The United States Army published a 5-Phase plan for raids that, like Mao's 3-Phase stratagem, is simple and broad yet specific enough to outline the most important actions to be taken:

Phase 1: Insert into the target area and establish a secure ORP

Phase 2: Seal off the area from outside support by using blocking and security elements. This is done by securing and observing all avenues that any reinforcements can come from

Phase 3: Any enemy force at or near the objective is overcome by surprise and violence, using all available resources for shock effect

Phase 4: Accomplish the mission before outside forces can arrive or be alerted

Phase 5: The force quickly withdraws to the ORP and then from the target area

Immediately after securing the site, supplies and intelligence should be gathered, situation permitting. For intelligence, the attacking force should quickly conduct Sensitive Site Exploitation (SSE) before withdrawing. SSE is the collection of anything that has the potential to yield intelligence, such as hard drives, cell phones, laptops, files, paperwork, photographs, and maps.

The timing and approach of the raid is also important. It is important to understand, as best as possible, the disposition of the defending forces, to best identify where and when the attacking force should begin the assault. Time of day, time of year, and weather are all factors that can be influential to the activities of the defending force. The attacking force may also consider approaching the target area from difficult or seemingly impassible terrain. This will add to the surprise and shock factor that should be used against the defending forces.

Throughout the duration of the raid, blocking and security elements of the raiding party should strive to keep the avenue of retreat secure, while also keeping watch for any enemy reinforcements. Their objective could be to keep the reinforcements away from the raid site entirely or it could be to simply observe their approach and alert the assault force, allowing them time to safely withdraw. The blocking elements should also withdraw as quickly as possible following completion of the raid. Just like ambushes, the size and objective of the blocking element(s) should be influenced by the terrain, availability of manpower, and what kind of firepower they have access to.

Additionally, a raid could be conducted against a mobile or semi-static target. For example, cartels in Mexico frequently conduct such raids by using a fast-moving convoy of two to four vehicles. The convoy would roll up to its target (often an idle vehicle at a red light, a gas station, or restaurant) and the shooters would dismount (or simply fire through the open windows), assault their target, and immediately flee. They have also been known to use such tactics for kidnappings. Such actions can be difficult to prevent because of how quickly they take place, and if the attack occurs on or near a busy roadway, then it would be nearly impossible for security forces to track or pursue the vehicles, especially if they split up. Similar tactics have been used in Asia, Latin America, and Africa, but with motorbikes and compact weapons, instead of heavily armed and organized convoys.

At its core, a raid is like an ambush in that it requires extreme surprise and violence of action to prevent the opposing forces from regaining their stability after initial contact. It is critical that unconventional groups use such tactics.

MOBILITY, COUNTER MOBILITY, & BORDERS

Another strength that guerrilla forces have is their ability to cover large distances in short amounts of time. This is usually accomplished through an intimate understanding of local and regional terrain and geography. Through area study and meticulous planning, guerrilla forces can take advantage of the opportunities that the terrain may hide from conventional forces, such as cave systems, intermountain passes, or shallow trails through a swamp. Guerrillas can see paths where conventional forces see obstacles.

Of course, the traditional mode of transportation for guerrillas is just walking. For thousands of years, militias and guerrilla forces walked for dozens of miles to get where they intended to go. Foot travel is extremely important, and so conditioning the legs, hips, shoulders, and back for extended activity with weighted packs should be a prime focus in training. Often, to help them go the distance, guerrillas would use pack animals to decrease their carrying load. The use of goats, donkeys, mules, horses, and llamas to carry food, supplies, water, ammunition, weapons, and wounded or captured fighters has been common throughout human history. Some pack animals, such as goats, are especially useful since they require little to no food besides what they forage for and can be used as a food source in case of emergency. To this day, it is not uncommon for guerrilla fighters to use pack animals when in difficult terrain, such as the Hindu Kush and the Caucuses. Pack animals are even sometimes used in recreational hiking throughout mountain ranges in the US and Europe. When trained well and used appropriately, guerrillas can use pack animals to increase their effectiveness, mobility, and longevity when in the field, especially when resupplies are few and far between.

A more recent development has been the use of light vehicles to move through or across difficult terrain. Dirt bikes and all-terrain vehicles have seen limited use since the mid-1900s but have recently seen extensive use by special forces in the middle east and Africa. The United States and Russia specifically have used dirt bikes and custom-built all-terrain vehicles to help insert into restricted areas and raid locations in Iraq and Syria. These types of vehicles can be low-vis and easier to conceal than the loud, slow, and usually up-armored vehicles conventional forces use. Guerrilla forces can, and occasionally have, used these types of vehicles to get around quickly, as they can be cached, muffled, and usually have fair ranges.

It is also possible to guerrillas to cover extensive distances using waterways. Lightweight canoes or kayaks can be cached and used to quietly navigate lakes and rivers, enabling guerrillas to avoid potentially surveilled roads and highways. Portaging can allow users of kayaks and canoes to move between bodies of water unnoticed.

While guerrilla forces are masters of mobility, they also have a strong understanding of counter mobility, that is, reducing the mobility of an opposing force. Guerrillas throughout history have used counter mobility, sometimes to devastating effect, against slower conventional forces. Counter mobility is usually a passive activity, such as cutting thick timber and laying it across an important roadway, destroying railways, digging and camouflaging anti-armor ditches along likely paths of approach, or even laying pressure-activated mines and IEDs to deny access to an area. However, counter mobility can also be an active activity, used during raids or ambushes to trap a force. Before an ambush, for example, the assault force may use axes or small explosive charges to fell trees and block the road, trapping a convoy of vehicles within a kill zone. In Vietnam and other conflicts, guerrilla forces would set fires to dry forests or grasslands (intentionally or unintentionally) to reduce the visibility and restrict the movement of a more conventional force. In Vietnam, it became difficult for gunships to deliver accurate fire on target due to the smoke. It also made ground forces hesitant to move. By limiting the capabilities and operational certainty of the conventional forces, it became a force multiplier for the guerrillas.

Counter mobility also has infrastructural and geographical aspects to it. Some things simply cannot be maneuvered through or around without great difficulty, and guerrilla forces can take advantage of that. For example, guerrillas in urban areas that have a high concentration of non-combatants typically have less concern for hostile heavy armor, artillery, or air power due to the risk of collateral damage (it should be noted that conventional forces are beginning to reduce the threat of collateral damage with the development and proliferation of extremely precise munitions, such as the AGM-114R Hellfire II and AGM-114R9X missiles and "smart bullets." Conventional forces may also clear an area by issuing an evacuation order or a shelter-in-place advisory before attacking). In areas where heavy conflict has already damaged the urban landscape, rubble and debris can be turned into obstacles. In urban environments, the role of weeding out guerrillas usually falls on intelligence gathering entities, special forces, and infantry.

Other barriers include natural geography such as bodies of water, mountains, and forests. These barriers prevent conventional forces from using assets that cannot operate in or around them. Thick forests prevent armor from driving through and can obscure aerial views. Bodies of water require amphibious or air transports to navigate and are sometimes restricted as to where a force can land based on terrain, tide, or other physical features. Weather can also be an obstacle. Russia, for example, is notorious for using its brutal winters to slow down or completely stop attacking forces. The extremely low temperatures and thick mud that builds up on unpaved roads can trap and has trapped conventional forces that are bogged down by logistics lines and support forces. In the case of the Battle of Takur Ghar, the knee-deep snow made it difficult for American forces to maneuver around the mountain, whereas Al-Qaeda forces hunkered down in an extensive series of caves and bunkers. High winds and low cloud cover reduce aircraft effectiveness and flight time. This is especially true for unmanned vehicles. Movements can be planned to coincide with incoming weather systems.

Counter mobility can be an intentional effort through the destruction or reinforcement of preexisting barriers. Burning forests, destroying dams, damaging runways, felling trees, or building roadblocks out of city rubble are all examples of intentional counter mobility.

Finally, guerrillas can use international or interstate borders against conventional military or police forces. The diplomatic situations and relationships of neighboring nations should be considered when borders are nearby. In the case of Afghanistan, it was very common for Al-Qaeda and Taliban fighters to cross into Pakistan to prevent U.S. forces from pursuing or conducting air strikes. Crossing into Pakistan also provided ample opportunity for recruiting, rest, and resupply. Taliban forces were able to leverage their relationship with the Pakistani ISI to gain intelligence and financing.

This tactic works often but could not always be relied upon. The U.S. occasionally crossed into Pakistan illegally to pursue and destroy fleeing fighters, often using either special forces or drones. Sometimes Pakistan would cooperate with the U.S. and conduct airstrikes or raids of their own, however Pakistan is notorious for harboring the groups and failing to effectively combat them.

This tactic was also used during the Vietnam war, where Viet Cong fighters would slip into Cambodia or Laos to prevent American ground forces from pursuing. They would also use rafts to float supplies along international rivers, oftentimes preventing American forces from destroying them. The task of pursuing the VC usually fell to the South Vietnamese Army, which, like Pakistan, was notorious for refusing to directly oppose the Viet Cong. Again, the U.S. still crossed these borders to pursue and destroy fleeing forces. The CIA ran numerous black operations in Laos and Cambodia to weaken the industrial and logistical base of the VC, such as Project Eldest Son, which was a program that sabotaged VC ammunition and ordnance. The CIA was also responsible for equipping, training, and organizing non-communist fighters in Laos to oppose the Viet Cong and the North Vietnamese backed Pathet Lao (the Laotian communist organization). Utilizing border-crossings and taking advantage of international political situations does not magically remove the risk of pursuit, but it does put the pursuers in a difficult position to either let guerrilla fighters escape or face potential political backlash which could then be further used against them.

Even outside of outright war, this tactic is used frequently. In the case of the Mexican cartels, they are known to flee across the US-Mexico border to prevent U.S. Customs and Border Patrol from pursuing. But, just as with the cases of Afghanistan and Vietnam, U.S. law enforcement has sometimes operated or conducted investigations in Mexico illegally, or, more commonly, with the permission or collaboration with Mexican authorities (even still, Mexican authorities often pass information on raids or investigations to cartels). This collaboration is especially common between stable governments. Official cross-border collaboration in Vietnam was not very viable due to the internal issues within Cambodia and Laos, as well as the legal and diplomatic restrictions the U.S. placed on itself (these, of course, did not prevent the CIA from conducting cross-border activities anyway).

There is an important factor that ties all these situations together. When moving across borders, militant groups use the known state of corruption and diplomatic red tape to prevent conventional forces from pursuing. These nations are usually politically or religiously aligned with the groups or are easily paid off to look the other way.

TACTICAL RETREATS AND SKIRMISHES

Retreating has always been a fundamental part of war. For a long time, many societies and forces had very aggressive and negative opinions about retreating. They viewed it as cowardly or even treasonous, and it sometimes was punished with summary execution, especially in the communist armies of the 20th century. Many of the greatest forces knew how to retreat to regroup and ultimately defeat the enemy. The Mongols, for example, were able to utilize their extreme mobility to conduct highly effective feigned retreats. For guerrillas, however, retreating is not such a controversial issue. In fact, it is necessary.

A general rule of thumb passed down by many of the greatest guerrilla strategists and tacticians, namely Sun Tzu and Che Guevara, is to engage briefly and withdraw until the enemy rests. The tactical retreat is conducted immediately following raids, ambushes, and skirmishes, so as the take advantage of the guerrilla's mobility and the conventional opponents lack of mobility. The tactical retreat has become even more important in the last century due to the proliferation of combat aircraft, and especially drones in the last 40 years. As time goes by, the loitering time of these weapons are increasing, allowing them to respond quickly and remain in an area for an extended amount of time. For guerrillas to attack a target and then immediately retreat from the site to a place where they are safe from observation and attack is imperative to their longevity.

It is unrealistic for a guerrilla to expect to be in a long, drawn-out engagement and come out on top. The reality is that conventional forces will begin orchestrating a combined response the moment contact occurs. Response teams will begin to deploy and cordon off any potential escape routes, helicopters and aircraft outfitted with high-powered zoom and thermal optics will enter the area and begin scanning for signatures from miles off, and direct-action teams will begin to pursue and either intercept the guerrillas or drive them into the cordon line. Staying in the area to fight is not a winning strategy, it is foolish. Objectives should be accomplished with haste and all effort should be put into immediately exfiltrating.

Now knowing the importance of a guerrilla force being able to avoid being drawn into a direct and lengthy confrontation, we can address *the skirmish*. A skirmish is a light battle, one that has few, if any, strategic implications. However, a skirmish can grow into a large and destructive battle very quickly. From the guerrilla's perspective, these should be avoided as much as possible. Every fighter that a guerrilla force can field is an important asset and losing fighters in strategically unimportant skirmishes can do significantly more damage to guerrilla forces than conventional ones. Conventional forces typically have little trouble fielding new fighters to replace their casualties, the opposite is true for guerrillas.

If a skirmish develops, then the guerrilla force should break contact immediately once the objective has been accomplished, or sooner if the objective cannot be completed. If the guerrilla force fails to withdraw from the skirmish, then it is possible that they may get dragged into a longer engagement than expected, allowing the conventional force to orchestrate reinforcements, air support, intelligence assets, or even artillery support against the guerrillas. The skirmish provides no benefits for the guerrilla, only risks. The guerrilla force should always seek to engage an enemy on its own terms or not at all. If a skirmish breaks out, and withdrawing is not an option, the guerrilla force should use every asset to overtake the opponent with extreme violence of action. Allowing a conventional foe to set the tempo for an engagement is a recipe for disaster, and the moment the balance starts to tilt in favor of the conventional force, the guerrilla force should seek to retreat and live to fight another day.

The rules for skirmishing also apply to ambushes and raids. Should ANY engagement reach a prolonged state of stagnation, or the guerrilla force is confident that enemy support (such as ground reinforcements or air support) has been or will be called in, then the guerrilla force should break contact and escape before they are forced into a state of stagnation and are fixed to a point. There is no shame in tactical retreat, and it is what keeps a guerrilla force going.

The ability to deceive an enemy that thinks in terms of classic conventional near-peer conflicts is a hallmark for guerrilla warriors. There are many ways for a guerrilla force to deceive an enemy, including movements (such as feigned retreats), information deception (deliberately feeding false information), and by manipulating the preconceptions and psychology of an opposing force.

One example of deception would be the Battle of Loudoun Hill during the First War for Scottish Independence, where Robert the Bruce used bogs and trenches to minimize the mobility and numerical superiority of the English forces, especially their cavalry. They also made their numbers appear smaller, until the British charged along the highway into the bog and militiamen raised pikes, rendering the English cavalry useless. Robert was able to devastate a superior military force through his deception. The English had destroyed Bruce's forces previously in battle and *expected* that any further pitched battle would be easily won, and that their fearmongering across Scotland would keep people from joining his army or lending him aid. Robert took advantage of their preconceptions by waging a guerrilla war until his forces were stronger and could fight conventional battles (again, Mao's 3-Phases) and it yielded dividends.

Whereas deception is a broad subject, one specific tool of deception that guerrillas tend to use often would be a feint. A feint is a type of deception in which the guerrilla force leads the opposing force to believe that a particular activity will happen, only to alter the expected result at the last minute. A feint can also involve deceiving the enemy into believing that a force has more capabilities than it really does. Feints can be offensive or defensive. They can be completed by feeding the opposing force information from a neutral source that indicates the weakness of the guerrilla force or by physically appearing to exist in a weakened state.

Examples of feints would be the use of "quaker guns" by the confederate army in the Civil War, used to indicate a stronger and more defended position than what is present. This altered battle planning, allowing more maneuverability for confederates and restricted planning for Union forces. Additionally, the great Mongol Strategist Subutai used feigned retreats to defeat the Kingdom of Georgia at the Battle of Khunan. Throwing their full weight at the Georgian line, the Mongols fought for a time and then feigned a panic and retreated, forcing the Georgians to break their own lines to pursue the Mongol party. This allowed a group of Mongols to ambush them from the flanks and destroy the Georgian army.

Successfully implementing feints and deception against the enemy allow guerrillas to even the playing field. Forcing the opponent to improperly employ their assets in the wrong place or at the wrong time will allow guerrillas to complete their objectives with less resistance.

URBAN & PERI-URBAN CONSIDERATIONS

In a modern world, it is impossible for a guerrilla force to operate exclusively out of the mountains. If they seek success, they need to operate within areas where the population is most concentrated. It is estimated that 56% of the world's population lives in cities, and that is expected to increase by 13% by 2050. This means that 7 in 10 people will live in cities. This trend of rapid, largely unplanned urbanization has many troubling implications, including more frequent and intense housing crises, resource scarcity, increasing amounts of violent organized crime, and food insecurity.

In America specifically, roughly 80% of the population lives in urbanized areas and this is only expected to increase, following the same trend as the rest of the globe. The entire Eastern Seaboard is almost one giant metropolitan area, with most counties having a metro area of considerable size. This inter-locking series of urbanized counties stretches almost uninterrupted (except for small sections of rural counties in North and South Carolina) from as far north as Androscoggin County, Maine to Miami-Dade County, Florida.

If the goal of the guerrilla is to conduct operations where they will be the most effective and will draw the most support, then it only makes sense that the guerrilla will operate not only in the mountains and forests, but also in the streets.

For us to understand how guerrillas can operate and succeed within the urban or peri-urban environment, we first must define these environments and then identify what makes them function.

Peri-urban (or *near* urban) environments are human settlements between rural territory and the densely populated urban centers. Examples of the peri-urban environment include suburbs and small to medium sized commuter towns. Peri-urban areas are less densely populated than urban areas and typically have less economic opportunity, requiring many to commute to urban areas for work, school, or access to other services, and then commute home. Many in peri-urban areas are blue collar workers, responsible for performing much of the labor and facilitation of day-to-day operations in the urban environment. These can be janitors, construction workers, IT system administrators, police officers, firemen, and nurses. It is often in peri-urban areas where utilities for the urban area will be found, such as landfills, power stations, arterial roadways and highways, and industrial areas such as factories and rail hubs.

The urban environment is an area of high population density and major infrastructure development, such as detailed highway systems, pronounced skylines, and unique neighborhoods. Urban environments, by nature, grow and expand due to the near constant increases in population. This expansion, called *urban sprawl*, puts undue stress on nearby peri-urban and rural areas, as they are now competing with the urban area for economic opportunity, resources, and land access. Urban sprawl can also put pressure on existing systems within the urban area, as the pre-existing systems now need to service a larger population. It is not uncommon for the immigration rate to exceed the pace of development, leading to underserved and often impoverished communities.

Cities and peri-urban environments are often described as living, breathing entities that require inputs and produce outputs. For both urban and peri-urban environments to function, there must be a stable flow of inputs and outputs. This is known as *urban metabolism*, a study system within the field of sociology. In the human body, our metabolism processes food and drink (inputs) into usable energy and waste (outputs). When there is an excess of inputs, and the "body" is unable to effectively process them into outputs and the result is metabolic dysfunction. Urban metabolism works in a very similar way. When the inputs (food, water, fuels, illicit goods, money, trade goods, immigrants, information, etc.) are not being processed effectively (due to a lack of capacity from rapid, unplanned urbanization) or the inward flow of these inputs is disrupted, then the result is once again metabolic dysfunction. This dysfunction materializes as violent crime, corruption, poverty, economic or social inequality, urban decay, and pollution.

Knowing these things, we can now look at urban and peri-urban environments through the lens of conflict. Disrupting the flow of inputs into the city inconveniences and distresses the civilian population. Naturally, the civilian population will oppose whoever they determine is responsible for the disruptions. During insurgencies, counterinsurgents typically restrict any activity that allows the city to "breathe" or "flow." Allowing the city to flow naturally, or at least at a normal capacity, creates opportunities for insurgents. Successful counterinsurgencies strike a balance between security operations (e.g., checkpoints on key roadways, raids, curfews, martial law, etc.) and allowing the civil government to operate with a degree of autonomy and guaranteeing freedom of movement for individuals and city inputs. Successful insurgencies, on the other hand, are not afraid of inconveniencing the civilian population. Instead, they look to shift the blame exclusively onto the counterinsurgents. The insurgency will act against the counterinsurgent force or the civil government, the counterinsurgency will respond with restrictive measures intended to isolate or restrict the insurgent, and the insurgency will work to convince the civilian population that the restrictions are oppressive and draconian. Whoever is able to convince the public that their cause is just (or at least that the opposing side is in the wrong) will usually enjoy a healthy degree of support.

This seemingly perpetual game of tug-of-war also has several micro-considerations. Each city responds to crime and conflict differently. Some respond with passive restrictions, monitoring situations and then responding quickly to any incidents. In London, for example, there are nearly 630,000 active CCTV cameras, or roughly one camera per 15 citizens. These cameras are rarely being monitored by a live person. They instead use highly advanced AI systems to constantly scan for high-value persons or threats, such as firearms or suspicious activities. Additionally, 90% of British police are unarmed. Once a significant threat is detected, either by a member of the public or by the gargantuan surveillance system across London, authorities deploy Authorized Firearm Officers (AFOs) who are trained in firearm usage, as well as any relevant counterterrorism teams to cordon off the area and raid locations. This system of detection and response is derived from England's monarchal history, with an emphasis on separating the military and any kind of martial activity from policing.

In the U.S., there is a very different response to shootings, terrorism, and civil disturbances. Most police are armed, and they routinely patrol the cities for civil disturbances, traffic violations, violent crimes, and calls from their dispatchers. Accordingly, interactions with police have the potential to evolve into confrontation. Since the SOPs of American police are so vastly different from their European counterparts, so to are they different in their responses to attacks and security operations. American police opt to inundate the immediate and surrounding area of a crime or attack with police, reducing the chance of the perpetrator(s) slipping out of the city. They will also lock down any means of egress, including highways, subways, bridges, airports, ports, rivers, and other waterways. Such SOPs are developed largely based on a city's physical geography. Coastal cities, like New York or Washington D.C., will naturally have a section of their police forces dedicated to patrolling and securing its waterways. Larger cities and county sheriffs will also respond using aircraft to patrol for suspects. Understanding how a certain city may respond to incidents could assist in mission and egress planning.

It is expected that any city will employ technologically superior assets to respond to incidents, whether it be aircraft to patrol the area, armored vehicles to transport tactical teams, or employing mass surveillance systems. In a rural environment, it becomes difficult for counterinsurgents and police forces to effectively employ their technological assets. Everything is spread out, so response times are exponentially slower than in cities. Rural areas also create a much larger area to observe or patrol, usually including difficult terrain that typical police might struggle to search or patrol. Through a basic survey of physical and social characteristics, it becomes clear how radically different a guerrilla force needs to operate between a city and the countryside. Despite these differences, it is extremely important that a guerrilla force operates out of both environments with equal intent while pursuing a unified strategy.

Now that the broad characteristic of the urban and peri-urban environments have been addressed, we can explore some of the more tactical considerations within these environments.

While there are numerous obstacles a group might face in a city, generally, there are only two broad concerns a guerrilla force must address. Those are:

- Getting INTO and OUT OF the city
- Operating WITHIN the city

Most often during conflicts, cities undergo strict regimentation, with measures like checkpoints, curfews, rationing, and increased patrols by military and police, leading to a heightened state of alertness and tension between authorities and civilians. For a guerrilla force to accomplish their goals, they need to take advantage of these tensions and be able to circumvent the security measures that a police force may implement.

In 1971, the RAND corporation released a paper by Brian Michael Jenkins, a counterterrorism expert, recognizing those 2 broad obstacles and detailing how a guerrilla force might be able to take over a city. In the paper, Jenkins describes a 5-stage process that he believes guerrilla forces could use.

1. <u>Violent Propaganda</u> – Where guerrilla forces conduct practical and symbolic acts of violence, such as small-scale assassination campaigns or destroying pro-government monuments/symbols. This is mostly to erode public confidence in the opposition's leadership and increase guerrilla morale.

2. <u>Organizational Growth</u> – This stage encourages more acts of propaganda, but also to weaken government forces and draw attention away from rural guerrillas. All activities within Stage 1 continue with increased tempo. Intelligence operations and influence campaigns are also conducted here to increase morale and recruitment efforts.

3. <u>The Guerrilla Offensive</u> – In this stage, the guerrilla force should be well-established and begin to conduct armed attacks, such as quick, low-to-medium risk raids and ambushes. During this stage, supplies should be massed and shared amongst fighters. Bombings and assassination campaigns on government, military, and police targets continue and become more frequent. Some guerrilla forces may be able to take over small, poorly controlled neighborhoods in this stage.

4. <u>Mobilization of the Masses</u> – This stage mandates that guerrilla forces encourage, enable, and organize protests and riots against government forces. Another tool that guerrillas can use to mobilize the masses is to showcase the violent government and military reprisals against guerrillas and civilians (such as strict curfews, unlawful detentions, or attacks resulting in collateral damage) to get the civilian population to turn against the government and instead support the incoming civil arm of the guerrilla force.

5. <u>Urban Uprising</u> – This is the end stage (like Mao's phase 3). The guerrillas should receive overwhelming support from civilians and the government forces and influence should be severely weakened. Rural guerrillas also enter the city in a final push, throwing out government forces and taking control of any critical locations,

such as police stations, government buildings, transit into and out of the city, and TV or radio stations.

It would be prudent to add a 6th stage to Jenkins' analysis.

6. <u>Solidify Control</u> – It is in this final stage that the guerrilla forces, now the dominant political force in the city, begin to implement their own policies. Governance should be turned over as soon as possible to a civil government with some degree of legitimacy (gained from public support) and friendly combat forces should assume a defense role. Focus should be placed on reconstructing the city and resuming everyday services to return the civilian population to a state of normalcy. Friendly forces should begin conducting extensive counterintelligence operations to root out any defectors, collaborators, assets, or agents. Hostile forces might, in turn, conduct their own guerrilla operations, focusing on eliminating or abducting new government figureheads, attacking key infrastructure, or destroying symbols of the new government. All gained territory should be consolidated from the center of the city outward (as cities and towns are often seen as the seat of legitimacy), and defensive operations should be conducted on the outskirts and peri-urban areas to prevent any loss of territory.

Che Guevara talks briefly about this 6th stage in his book *Guerrilla Warfare*, speaking specifically about keeping and maintaining any power that has been won from the government forces. Solidifying control is about preventing government forces from re-establishing control over any territory, but also about dismantling or reforming any corrupt and tyrannical institutions that allowed the government to oppress. It is also important for the guerrillas to begin developing their own institutions, beginning with establishing a free, civilian-led government, and gradually expanding to other things such as encouraging free economic activity and an independent media. Civil affairs operations are still extremely important at this stage, just as with all other stages. Guerrillas may even open Civil Affairs offices to extend outreach and help the civilian population rebuild and prosper.

Jenkins' paper, while providing brilliant insight, only grapples with the task of securing a single city, rather than in a country, state, or region with dozens or even hundreds of cities. Should a single city fall, opposition government forces will not simply chalk it up as a loss. Instead, they will begin conducting their own insurgency campaign of intelligence operations, assassinations, and terrorism, and the guerrilla forces should be prepared for this. Opposition forces may even begin conducting air strikes or direct conventional operations to re-invade and eliminate the new government. The new government should be able to anticipate what actions the conventional opposition might take, and they should be immediately prepared for and countered.

While it is clear how Jenkins' and Mao's systems are similar, it is also jarring to see how they are different. To paraphrase Jenkins, everything is faster and more violent in cities. Groups should be tightly knit, highly intelligent, and cooperative as government responses are rapid and surgical. Guerrillas operating in urban environments need to understand how to fight government forces with a savage, extreme degree of violence, while also painting themselves as oppressed, peace-loving freedom fighters. If they are unable to do this, then they will slowly lose support, either being considered by the civilian population as wholly impotent or bloodthirsty criminals. The government and media outlets will begin labelling them as terrorists that are simply hellbent on violence and chaos. If this happens, and the government forces establish or re-establish trust with and control over the public in opposition to the guerrillas, it is likely that any future attempt for guerrillas to access the city will result in failure.

Jenkins' 5 stages, like Mao's 3-Phases, are broad, but each provide specific steps that should be followed or constraints to exist within. The stages of Jenkins' system follow roughly the same process of Mao's, by starting small, building up the organization, and taking symbolic actions to broaden support. Eventually ending with a final, massive assault against government forces.

COLLATERAL DAMAGE

As it has been discussed at length in this work as well as countless others, any self-respecting guerrilla should understand that their success rests on the will of The People. Without the support of the common man, there is no hope. So, during any conflict, a fighter should be constantly aware of the public's disposition, needs, and wants. However, in every conflict, there is the risk that innocent people, noncombatants, will be caught between government forces and guerrillas. Guerrillas themselves should avoid this at all costs. Harming noncombatants is not just morally wrong but will create major strain between the guerrilla force and the public. Historically, guerrilla forces have known this, and successful groups have avoided it to a great degree (it is virtually impossible to eliminate the risk of collateral damage). But some groups have discovered that repressive government responses to guerrilla activity can drive civilians into the arms of guerrilla fighters.

For example, on November 21st, 1920, Irish Republican Army operatives, on orders from Michael Collins, began simultaneously raiding rooming houses across Dublin. In these rooming houses were high level members of what was known as the *"Cairo Gang,"* plainclothes ex-military intelligence officers working to undermine the IRA in Dublin. The IRA operatives killed 15 people in total, including at least 1 civilian, but mostly intelligence officers. Throughout the raids, IRA operatives were also able to search the rooms of the intelligence officers and they retrieved a significant amount of intelligence. They planned the raid with intelligence given freely from Irish servants in the rooming houses and informants within the Irish and British intelligence services. Some operatives used lookouts to report the approach of any security forces. This was one of the most successful counterintelligence operations conducted in modern times, specifically because Michael Collins and other leaders within the Old IRA knew exactly how to operate within the urban landscape. The same day of the operation, there was a major soccer game being held, the proceeds of which went to a pro-republican charity fund. While the British and Irish security forces searched for the perpetrators of the raids, they decided to lock down the soccer match in hopes of finding the attackers somewhere in the crowd. They blocked the exits and were instructed to search all males leaving the game. Instead, they opened fire on the crowd for over a minute, shooting at fleeing, unarmed civilians. 14 noncombatants were killed (including 3 children and 1 woman), dozens more were injured. This massacre was condemned internationally and reinforced the disdain that many in Ireland had for the British. IRA recruitment swelled in response to the massacre.

While the raids themselves were a tactical military success, they had no major long term effect. The British still had significant control of Dublin and had begun rebuilding their intelligence networks fairly soon after. It was the repressive measures, and, specifically, the Bloody Sunday massacre, that helped the IRA win Irish independence. It is important to note, however, that the IRA did not relish in the idea of British forces indiscriminately killing innocents, but it is a tactic that works and can be used sparingly. Guerrillas should never openly encourage the killing or harm of innocent people, but should always highlight such tragedies when perpetrated by the opposition.

ARCHITECTURE AND THE BUILT ENVIRONMENT

Cities should be looked at like puzzles. They are large and can be overwhelming, but just like a puzzle, there are always patterns, contours, borders, and shapes that can be identified and exploited. Burglars do this regularly, especially professionals who case and take down major institutions like banks. They examine the space for days, weeks, months, sometimes years, and they find ways to manipulate the space to work to their advantage.

For example, Los Angeles has a highway system unlike any other. The sheer size of the highway system, the vast population of Los Angeles County, and the rugged surrounding areas around the city make it difficult for police to effectively patrol the entire region. The massive highway system has enabled petty criminals to easily escape, especially since there are many businesses and banks located at or near the highway on-ramps. However, this same system is what caused the LAPD to develop the world's largest police helicopter fleet. These helicopters loiter in certain areas and respond to crimes as necessary, reducing the strain on ground-based responders while also acting as an airborne command-and-control, organizing manhunts and reporting on suspect movements. This has not stopped criminals from using the highway systems to escape.

Los Angeles also has an extensive network of underground canals and storm drains that were paved over throughout the years. In the 1980s, a group known as the Hole-in-the-Ground gang took advantage of these tunnels and hit multiple banks throughout L.A. Instead of walking through the front door, masks on and guns in hand, they attacked from below, a direction that no one could have expected. Using the storm drains and tunnels beneath the banks, they came in from below and hit the vault and deposit boxes. They dammed the canal and released it every time they left to wash away any evidence into the L.A. River. They used ATVs to escape through the tunnels, and the men who bought the ATVs were nondescript white males wearing construction clothing, such as a high-visibility vests and jeans (hardly the attire of hardened criminals). The gang has never been caught. Professionals like them look at all avenues of approach within an urban environment, including those that go beyond the use of doors. They drill through floors, access rooftops, and punch holes through walls. They access nearby abandoned buildings to scout out the area, and they use the repetitive layout of corporate chain buildings to simplify their approaches. They use social engineering to pretend to be someone they are not and convince the unwitting employee to give them access they should not have. They mentally map out rooms and security systems to copy down later to further study and burn into their minds.

Every city, from the largest metropolitan centers to the homey small towns, has a set of qualities. These qualities are sometimes unique, such as Los Angeles's highways and canals, New York City's extensive metro network, or Venice's canals. However, most cities are designed in grids, and patterns can be found within. If any group is operating within an urban environment, it would be prudent to study the environment as closely as possible before taking any action.

THE URBAN CROWD

Urban guerrilla warfare has a storied past, dating back thousands of years to the first civilizations. The Jewish Sicarii, mentioned earlier for their 3-year resistance and subsequent mass-suicide at Masada, operated extensively in urban environments, especially in Jerusalem. They got their name from the dagger they carried, and their standard practice for killing romans, roman sympathizers, and basically anyone else who was not a zealot. During public events, they would slip through the crowd with their cloaks on and approach their targets. All at once, they would draw their blades and attack their targets simultaneously before escaping with the crowd in the chaos. This tactic often caused severe retribution from the Romans and was partially responsible for the destruction of Jerusalem in 70 CE. Any security force, whether it be local police or Roman legions, will burn down everything if it becomes completely impossible to tell friend from foe.

This same tactic was that the Sicarii used to escape was likely used during the Bloody Sunday massacre. The IRA almost certainly intentionally used the early morning crowds to escape detection, and the British security forces even supposedly found discarded firearms at the scene of the massacre. Hiding in crowds acts as a sort of shield (most of the time). It can prevent detection and cause security forces to hold their fire. This, of course, is not a perfect tactic. At any time, security forces can open fire and wound or kill innocent people. At any time, the blame can shift from the security forces to the guerrillas, and the same strategy that worked for the Old IRA could be the downfall of another group. Context matters.

Crowds can be used in non-combat situations as well, and this is more permissible as the risk of violence and retribution against civilians is low. Using crowds, even simply blending in with other civilians at public events, can allow an agent of a guerrilla force to gather intelligence. Burglars use this often when staking out a target, posing as a passerby or a commuter, an artist or a tourist.

CLANDESTINE CELLS

As mentioned during the discussion about Jenkins' 5-step process for urban guerrilla warfare, once a city is placed on alert and police begin to control the flow in and out of cities, it will be extremely difficult for a guerrilla force operating in rural environments to insert into the city, accomplish an objective, and escape. This means that a guerrilla force needs to insert a cell of fighters and intelligence operatives into a city before it begins Phase 2 of Mao's rural system. When Phase 2 begins, and the security of the surrounding cities is heightened, there will be no need to insert teams of fighters, as they are already inside. This practice of preemptive deployment can also help combat counterinsurgency operations (which will be explored in a later chapter).

These cells should be deployed with ample time to establish working identities for themselves before any major hostilities begin. They must appear to be normal citizens with a demonstratable history of income, residence and social relationships. They should have jobs to work, bills to pay, and personal relationships to cultivate. Communication with the guerrilla force on the outside should be minimal to nonexistent. They should appear to have ***ZERO*** political or social ties to the guerrilla group, as even the slightest association can attract attention from state security or intelligence agencies. Any attention is too much, in this case. They may remain in contact with other members of their cell within the city, or they may not. That decision is situation dependent. If they elect not to remain in contact with each other, then there should be a place where they can meet in case of emergency or activation. This place can be public, such as a coffee shop or a gym, but it may also be private or secluded, such as an abandoned warehouse or a rented motel room. Again, these decisions are situational, and discretion should be used when making them. It is important that no reference to the location ever be made in writing.

These cells could be activated by a signal or a codeword hidden in plain sight (notice of activation could be a non-descript advertisement in a local paper using a key word or phrase, for example). Again, any attention is too much attention. The activation signal could also be a preestablished event (such as an election or holiday), a date, or a time. Once the cells are activated, they should move to accomplish whatever objective(s) they were assigned prior to deployment. All the details surrounding their mission, their covers, etcetera should have been planned, explained, and understood before deployment. Once the time comes to execute, there should be no knowledge gap preventing them from accomplishing the mission they were assigned.

Should an emergency arise, such as a setback in the plan or if the cell is breached by security or intelligence services, there should be a general guideline for the members of the cell to follow. Rendezvous points should be established and plans to escape the city and reintegrate into the main guerrilla force should be developed in advance. Of course, extreme caution should be observed to avoid leading state security or intelligence organizations directly back to outside forces. A period of observation should occur, and counterintelligence efforts made before any attempt to reintegrate with the main force. Should the emergency not warrant the evacuation of the cell, then they should simply remain put. If the mission becomes untenable (that is, accomplishing the assigned objective(s) is no longer something that is possible within reason) then the cell should follow their established protocol to evacuate and reintegrate.

As objectives for the cell may vary, one mission they may be assigned to is to insert into a city and develop an internal guerrilla force that is physically separate from the main guerrilla body while retaining the same identity and strategic goals of the main body (this internal group should *NOT* be a splinter group with its own goals and identity). If this is the goal, then the main guerrilla body should develop a logistics system to supply the cell within the city. This means smuggling in supplies and arms until the internal cell can sustain themselves. Once the internal force is self-sustaining, then the flow of supplies from the outside-in should be suspended. This is one of the instances where low intensity raids, ambushing, and 3D printing can become beneficial. Once the internal guerrilla force begins its implementation of the Jenkins 5-Step system, then it will begin to draw the attention of government forces, taking pressure off the rural guerrillas. Once the rural guerrillas then are given the opportunity to shore up their own gains, they will eventually be able to come to the aid of the urban guerrillas, unite, and accomplish phase 5 together.

This relationship between the urban and rural guerrillas is symbiotic in nature. They should seek to support each other wherever possible, whenever possible. Their tactical objectives are different, but their strategic objective of deposing a despotic government and installed a new, agreed upon governing body is something they can unify around. The successes of one are the successes of the other, as are the failures and setbacks. Should either force fail, then the government will be unrestricted in their pressure on the remaining force. This could be catastrophic for the organization, and directly jeopardizes the guerrilla war effort. Both groups need to exist in a constant state of operational harmony if they seek to accomplish a unified strategic goal.

SAFE HOUSES

Safe houses are secure locations where guerrilla fighters can hide, recuperate, and prepare for operations. There are certain requirements that safe houses and their surrounding areas should have before any steps are taken to inhabit or operate out of it.

Safe houses should be changed often. The exact lifespan of a safe house is debatable as there are several factors that determine its usability. This period could range from a few days to a few months, depending on the activities that are being conducted from within and the suspicions of authorities. The location should not be obvious, such as a top floor apartment or a house on the corner of the street. Any inhabitants should limit movement in or out, as neighbors could report strange activities coming from the safehouse and inadvertently (or advertently) alert authorities. Additionally, any outside connections (phone, internet, etc.) should be policed heavily. Power consumption should not be suspect.

Safe houses should be defensive in nature, rarely offensive. The success of a safehouse lies in its ability to hide a group, as well as provide an early warning for the inhabitants should government forces discover their location. There should be sightlines within or near the safehouse that can observe approaches, such as roads, rivers, and the airspace. There should also been avenues of escape. Obvious avenues, such as roads or rivers, will almost certainly be monitored. Most police forces, when raiding a location, will lock down the surrounding area before beginning their approach. This area could consist of a single street or several city blocks. When planning escape routes, all options should be left on the table.

Planners should also consider creating new routes that security forces are not able to account for, such as tunnels leading to buildings suspected to be abandoned, occupied by friendlies or civilians, or leading directly out of the area. Depending on the location and the capabilities of the police, there may also be helicopter support to help coordinate the search. These factors, and more, should be considered before establishing a safe house. If the guerrilla forces have agents within the police forces or have scouts watching police stations and other locations that state forces may deploy from, they may be able to receive an early warning when the police begin to mobilize. Any force utilizing a safe house should be ready to move immediately, with little to no warning, and escape routes should be well-known but also compartmentalized as necessary.

Fighting should not be the main concern in this case. In the case that the safehouse is discovered, all inhabitants should focus on egressing and re-organizing.

For any mission or operation, appropriate planning prior to deployment is critical for operational success. Mission planning allows each team member to assess the capabilities of themselves and the team, prepare any relevant intelligence or equipment, recite or practice any technical aspects of the mission, and determine the most effective course of action to tackle the objective. The benefits of planning beforehand are clear, and it can improve team interoperability and success.

Mission planning is a rather linear process, outlining a series of steps and tasks that need to be followed and completed to provide leadership and team members with the most information to make effective decisions during the planning phase. Planning also reduces much of the guesswork and on-the-fly decision making during the operation.

STEP 1: RECEIPT OF MISSION

The planning process begins with an operational directive from leadership. In an unconventional organization, tactical decentralization is key but operational and strategic leadership should still exist (more on leadership in a later chapter). Leadership will have identified an operational need that the team must address. In the tasking, the operational goal(s) of the mission will be outlined, leaving the tactical decision making up to the team. Team members should be given the flexibility to use their own professional discretion in how the operational goal is met.

STEP 2: MISSION ANALYSIS

In the mission analysis, the team leader will complete several tasks. They will:

- Analyze the intent of the tasking (what is the goal of the tasking?)

- Determine the area of operations, identify relevant terrain, and develop a weather report (where will the operation take place? what is the physical geography?)

- Form threat assessments against current intelligence (what threats are in the area and what assets do they have available?)

- Orchestrate any available and relevant team members, assets, and resources

- Assess any civil considerations (local population, traffic, level of support, demographics, ASCOPE-PMESII)

In this step, leaders and decision makers will begin developing COAs to accomplish the intended objectives by analyzing the objective itself and incorporating intelligence on hostiles, civil considerations, weather, terrain, available team members and assets.

Each COA should be:

- <u>Feasible</u>: Realistically accomplishable within known constraints

- <u>Acceptable</u>: Benefits should outweigh the risks of the operation

- <u>Suitable</u>: The COA should accomplish the stated objective

Each COA should be run against the key criteria passed down from leadership. Criteria for each COA could be:

- <u>Surprise</u>: The ability for the team(s) to move in and out of the AO without alerting hostile forces or third parties

- <u>Flexibility</u>: The ability for the team(s) to react to unexpected circumstances and develop contingency plans

- <u>Intelligence Gathering</u>: Criteria for operational success could be for the team(s) to obtain specific intelligence regarding a predetermined matter

- <u>Speed</u>: The Ability for the team(s) to insert, complete the objective, and extract within a strict window of time

Each COA should be assessed for feasibility and checked to see if it meets the criteria handed down from leadership.

STEP 5: COA SELECTION & ORDER PRODUCTION

Leadership will be presented with the COAs that are (1) the most feasible, (2) accomplish all or most of the key criteria, and (3) have an optimal risk-reward ration. Once leadership is briefed on each COA, they will need to decide on which COA to approve. Once the COA is decided, orders will be issued, and the team(s) will begin preparing and rehearsing for the operation.

The mission planning process must determine how the team(s) will accomplish their objectives within the known environmental and criteria constraints. Mission planners and leadership should make a best effort to streamline the process based on their operational context.

SUBTERRANEAN ACTIVITIES

Guerrillas thrive in environments dominated by speed, surprise, and freedom of movement. However, in some cases the situation requires the guerrilla force to slow down and operate from a centralized location that can sustain the guerrilla force. Above ground structures can offer a false sense of security, no matter how fortified they may be. Over the last several decades, western counterinsurgent forces have honed their tactics against fortified structures housing suspected fighters. Several tier 1 units throughout the western world have been developed specifically to respond to urban insurgencies and fortified structures. In the end, even if the building can not be taken for some reason, the counterinsurgent forces reserve the ability to simply level the structure. To make the best of these circumstances, the guerrilla force can take their hub below the surface.

For centuries, guerrillas and disadvantaged forces have used tunnels, trenches, caves, and cavities to increase their capabilities against their enemies. Tunnels have been used to dig under enemy positions, such as walls or trenches, and either infiltrate the other side or detonate explosives under enemy positions. Additionally, tunnels and trenches have been used to escape from besieged positions using connector tunnels. The tunnels and trenches used to infiltrate and exfiltrate are often not found until they have been used, allowing the guerrillas to move with a large degree of freedom in and out of combat.

Trenches

Trenches are relatively simple to construct. The trench would be dug to varying specifications (depending on available construction time and resources) but typically deep enough for men to stand in (at least 6 feet deep) and wide enough for two men to pass each other. If needed, the walls were then shored up with wood panels, logs, or sandbags to prevent any loose dirt or mud from spilling back into the trench. If time and resources permitted, wood paneling would be placed on the ground to reduce the risk of trench foot from standing water and mud. Design specifications also changed based on the soil type. Soft or loose soils that held plenty of water, like clay, and soils that had very fine particles, like sand, absolutely had to be shored up to prevent refilling. Firmer soils like loam required less work and less fortifying and would likely harden itself during colder months.

For centuries, the trench existed in a state of stagnation. It was simple to build and there was not any need for innovation. This changed, however, with the development and proliferation of balloons and aircraft. During the American Civil War, balloons were used to float over entrenched positions. When the aeronaut (balloon pilot) reached an adequate height, they would then sketch the enemy positions and return to friendly lines for the maps to be studied. Battle plans would then be developed based on the layout of the trench system and the suspected manpower within. This led to changes in the layouts and usage of the trench systems, such as using overhead camouflage to mask troop numbers or movements and encouraged the construction of underground dugouts for forward headquarters, field kitchens, hospital relay points, and bunk rooms.

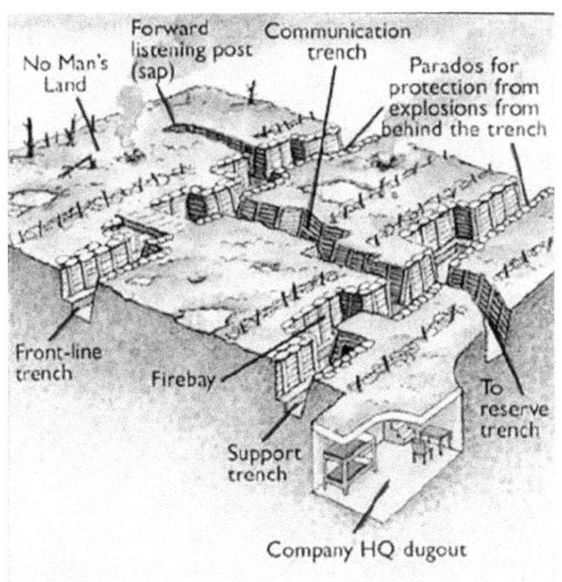

(A typical trench system, before the proliferation of aircraft)

Today, with reconnaissance aircraft and drones being so common on the battlefield, trenches must be heavily camouflaged. In the 2022 Russo-Ukrainian war, trenches have seen heavy usage. Drones are used to reconnoiter the trench system, reporting back troop numbers, capabilities, and allowing the pilot to map out the trench system. In response, trench defenders would camouflage the trench with local vegetation, timber, earthworks, and netting. The goal of these things is not necessarily to hide the existence of the trench, but to reduce the signatures emitted by the defenders. Once camouflaged, trench defenders can construct bunkers, dugouts for various facilities, and passageways to facilitate rapid ingress or egress in the event of an attack on the trench.

Trenches are useful in all environments, from urban centers to mountaintops. However, trenches shine the most on flat, grassy, or forested terrain. In flat environments, it is difficult to operate against conventional forces due to the lack of difficult terrain, cover, or concealment. Conventional forces can utilize the flat terrain to move quickly with mechanized infantry, airborne troops, aircraft, and drones. Ideally, the guerrilla would simply elect to not fight in such an environment. However, if the enemy is given the opportunity to dictate the location of the fight, the guerrilla could construct expedient trenches with the goal of escaping to a nearby area with more concealment, such as a town or forest. Sitting in one location for too long will result in the conventional force surrounding the site, saturate the area with troops, and coordinate assets such as air or artillery against the position. At this point it would be prohibitively difficult to achieve any kind of ideal outcome.

Trenches, due to their often linear nature, are perfect for ambushes and booby traps. Ambushing abandoned trenches is a very common tactic. Grenades set with tripwires would be placed in path junctions or doorways. Toe poppers (low yield explosive charges, usually pressure activated, that blow off toes or feet when hit) are placed in trench paths to slow the enemy advance and encumber their medical teams. Other times, the defenders would only pretend to have abandoned the trench, just to counterattack, drive the attackers back into the open, and kill them.

Trenches certainly have a long history of use and due to their versatility and effectiveness at protecting and concealing infantry, they will have an even longer future. Guerrillas and conventional forces alike can make use of trenches during times where movement is restricted. Making an enemy force focus on clearing a trench can free up other friendly forces to harass or attack other targets, potentially giving the trench defenders a window to escape. Usage will only increase as the guerrilla moves further into the 21st century.

Tunnels

Tunnels are much more complex than trenches, requiring precise engineering to avoid cave-ins. Additionally, enemy forces could block off tunnel entrances and exits. In some historical cases (such as during the Sino-Japanese War), attackers can deploy tear gas and other chemical weapons into the tunnels via entrances, exits, and air vents. Tunnels can also be flooded, or air access denied, drowning or suffocating the defenders. Because of all these drawbacks, tunnels are not expedient defensive positions. Any tunnels should be designed and constructed long before they are needed, to guarantee that escape passages are developed well in advance of them being needed.

The benefits of tunnels, however, may outweigh the risks. Tunnels make most observation completely impossible, especially from the air. Because of this, it also becomes extremely difficult to map out a tunnel system, whereas a trench can simply be followed until it ends. Tunnels give insurgents, guerrillas, and other disadvantaged fighters the ability to move with an unparalleled degree of freedom. They may also store supplies and munitions or move between cities, settlements, or individual buildings to ambush or escape counterinsurgent forces. Tunnels give guerrillas the opportunity to develop their own headquarters, complete with services such as an intelligence apparatus or a logistics corp. Such a location could be a strong morale boost, giving unconventional fighters a safe place to rest, recover, eat, and prepare. Of course, any static installation can be extremely dangerous for a guerrilla force, no matter how fortified or hidden. Tunnels may also be used for smuggling between borders or under defensive structures like walls.

As previously stated, tunnels can be difficult to develop safely. Cave-ins are a major threat, and so strong supports should be a primary focus during construction. Supports can be installed using wooden beams or poured concrete and rebar. The tunnel itself can be dug out manually using shovels and pickaxes, but also (If the situation permits) heavy equipment like excavators. The easiest way to construct a tunnel is called the cut-and-cover method. This is done by digging a trench, installing sturdy supports and a ceiling that can handle the overhead load, and then cover the trench with earth. Of course, there will be signs of construction and soil disturbance, so sod can be rolled over the surface or grasses (especially wild grasses or other natural vegetation, if the situation calls for it) can be sewn on the surface. This method can be more accessible because it reduces the amount of weight that is bearing down on the tunnel, thus reducing construction time, costs, and risk. Of course, the closer to the surface the tunnel is, the more likely it is to be discovered, either through happenstance or through intentional search, so any outbound signals or other emissions (such as radio communications, heat from cooking, or audible emissions from speech or movement) should be policed as necessary.

Additionally, tunnels can be constructed in urban environments using pickaxes and electric jackhammers. Hamas has constructed dozens of miles of tunnels throughout Gaza and into Israel, and most of these tunnels are under densely populated urban centers. Tunnels are the key to Hamas' war against the Israeli Defense Force. Hamas uses the tunnels to infiltrate Israel, to transport fighters to or away from battle, and to hide their vast arsenal of homemade rockets. One consideration for urban tunnels is to avoid hitting service lines, such as those transporting power, water, internet, or sewage. Any interruption will prompt investigation and result in the tunnel being discovered, so proper planning is especially important in urban environments. The sound of construction can also give away the defenders, so tunnel construction should only be done during periods of high surface activity, such as afternoon traffic, construction, or during the lunch rush.

For tunnels, air access and quality are of equal importance to structural integrity. Of course, without air, the defenders will simply suffocate in their system. Air shafts should be installed throughout the tunnel system to provide fresh air for anyone inside. These shafts should be camouflaged on the surface, as discovery could lead to attacks against the tunnel, including the destruction of the shaft or the deployment of chemical agents. Water access, also, is important. Wells can be dug, or pipes can be run from the surface to provide water for drinking, cooking, and waste. Of course, any sign of surface water collection should be sufficiently camouflaged.

Examples of successful tunnels are the Cu Chi tunnels of Ho Chi Minh City, the Sarajevo Tunnel under the Sarajevo International Airport, and the vast tunnel systems of Iwo Jima. All examples provided defenders incredible freedom of movement for moving fighters, non-combatants, and supplies. In some cases, the tunnels were used to connect intricate systems of bunkers and fighting positions, such as those at Iwo Jima.

PSYCHOLOGICAL OPERATIONS

In the final days of the Taliban offensive of 2021, the Taliban used social media to an extreme degree of success. So much so did they blow a major psychological coup against the ANA. While the United States pulled up stakes, restricted critical air support and CASEVACs from the defending Afghan commandos and began the withdrawal from Hamid Karzai International Airport (HKIA), the Afghans began receiving phone calls and text messages from the Taliban. In these text messages, the Taliban shared detailed, sensitive information that they knew about the commandos, mostly gathered from social media. Their current locations and identities, their family members, and where they called home were all shared in these messages. The threat of the Taliban showing up on a commando's doorstep was a crushing weight to bear. Along with the knowledge that the American air support was withdrawing, many members of the

ANA went into hiding or surrendered, and many of the major towns and cities along the route to Kabul were seized with very little, if any, fighting.

This was a psychological coup for the Taliban. Sun Tzu teaches:

"The supreme art of war is to subdue the enemy without fighting."

Psychological operations should serve the purpose of demoralizing, shocking, or otherwise weakening the enemy force. Examples can be showing photos of captures supplies, showing captured fighters and their confessions, or producing effective media showcasing the friendly forces capabilities. ISIS produced plenty of media that sparked fear in many, and inspired others to travel to Iraq and Syria to fight for the would-be caliphate.

Ideally, any produced media should be publicly available. This would influence the enemy forces but would also cause the public to cast doubt on the enemy's capabilities or response to the propaganda. This pressure can cause the civilians to reduce their faith in the counterinsurgency and place more faith into the guerrillas. Creating a decay in the trust between counterinsurgents and the public is a prime directive of guerrilla warfare.

Other examples of psychological warfare are the circulation of digital media depicting dead soldiers. This media is circulated online or can be delivered in targeted campaigns, such as what the Taliban did towards Afghan commandos. Ukraine has done this with great results in the 2022 Russo-Ukrainian war, where they would post photos of dead Russian soldiers on Russian social media sites, such as VK and Odnoklassniki, as well as western social media like WhatsApp, Instagram, and TikTok. They would also use captured cell phones to call the families or comrades of dead Russian soldiers. Such activities could causes extreme psychological harm, especially for would-be recruits and the war effort on the home-front.

Today, psychological operations occur largely online. The term "fake news" is directly derived from the attempt to combat psychological operations. Oftentimes, social media will be used to distort reality. Truth is called lies, lies are called truth, claims are made and backed up by flimsy (or solid) proof. The goal is not to convince the other side to change their minds. It is instead to cast doubt on the reality that they know. In doing so, they are weakened, their loyalties are challenged, and the information warfare capabilities of the enemy are reduced.

All these goals can be met, and more, by deploying the tactics and tools discussed in Chapter 4. Using the proper message, combined with a solid delivery, can shake the confidence that conventional armies have in their wars against small, unconventional groups.

In some cases, a successful guerrilla force may receive foreign aid. There are a few exceptions to this, namely the Bolshevik forces during the Russian Civil War and the Chinese communists in the Chinese Civil War. They are excluded due to the unique nature of their fight, their geography, and their strong political base, which allowed them to mobilize millions of peasants. For most other groups, however, they can receive either material, political, or financial support from foreign powers and political or social groups.

Foreign aid is gained through direct diplomacy. Identifying powers with strategic or political goals that align with one's group is key to finding allies who could provide material, financial, or political support. These diplomatic talks are usually covert and low level, as discovery that diplomatic talks are ongoing could destroy the opportunity before it becomes fully realized. Additionally, groups should strongly consider who they receive aid from, as such relationships can be and often are used in the propaganda campaigns of the opposition.

One example of foreign support would be the Peninsular War, in which there was the first documented use of the world Spanish word *Guerrilla*. After France had occupied Spain, the United Kingdom lent aid to Spain from 1808 until wars end in 1814. The English provided arms, supplies, and eventually invaded the Iberian Peninsula to help the Spanish and Portuguese forces. During the American Revolutionary War, it is known that France eventually lent military aid, but France, along with Spain, the Netherlands, and other European powers that opposed English hegemony assisted the Americans with loans, grants, arms, and political support. However, it was the direct military aid of France, the organizational assistance of Prussian officer Friedrich Wilhelm von Steuben, and the diplomatic savvy of Benjamin Franklin, that allowed the colonists to form their own nation. Had it not been for the extensive support of foreigners, it is unlikely that America would have been founded at that time.

Then, of course, there is the Provisional IRA, which received a considerable degree of weapons and financial assistance from the Irish American communities dotting the American Northeast, as well as from the sympathetic Libyan regime of Muammar Gaddafi. Irish nationalism was strong even within those Irish American communities, and they helped raise funds in America for the war effort in Ireland, often at great risk to themselves, as the American government was closely allied with Britain and began trying and punishing some of the Irish American organizers. Irish nationalist publications were also banned from the mail system, limiting, at the time, who could see them.

There is also the Arab Revolt against the Ottomans, in which the British and French lent material aid as well as advisors to the Arab and Bedouin forces. It was in this conflict that one of the most prolific guerrilla leaders would come to be known, T.E. Lawrence. If not for the European aid, the Arabs and Bedouins would have been crushed and the Ottoman Empire may not have fallen.

Despite the many success stories, foreign aid it not a magic bullet. Throughout the World Wars and the Cold War, hundreds, perhaps thousands, of guerrilla groups who received some degree of foreign aid either failed or were exterminated (mostly in Eastern Europe and Latin America). This was especially true under German and Soviet rule. No guerrilla force in the Soviet Union made any real impact in dislodging Soviet power. Some groups under Nazi rule were able to weaken infrastructure or provide intelligence for invading forces, but their impact was also limited. A combination of factors determines whether the group will be successful, foreign aid is only one of many tools that can be used.

A force multiplier is a factor or tool that increases the effectiveness of a force, essentially reducing the need for numerical or technological superiority. Unconventional groups must use force multipliers at every opportunity. Naturally, guerrillas are at a distinct disadvantage to their conventional opponents, and so they are forced to use force multipliers to succeed.

A force multiplier can be tangible or intangible, a concept, an idea, or a weapon. For example, strong morale can be a force multiplier, but so can a new crew served weapon. Weather, if used correctly, can be a force multiplier, as the Russians have done for centuries. Advanced training is a force multiplier. A next generation strike aircraft is a force multiplier. Experience can be a force multiplier. Mobility, which the guerrilla should be a master of, is also a force multiplier. Automatic weapons, mortars, or explosives can be force multipliers. Having a strong intelligence or counterintelligence apparatus is a force multiplier.

Force multipliers should be identified and exploited as identified. This is a rule that both guerrillas and conventional armies should live by. If it increases the effectiveness of the overall force, then it is something that should be explored and pursued.

DRONES

In recent years, the proliferation of drones has exceeded the expectations of many. Drones as we understand them have been in use since the Cold War. In the 1980s and '90s, the CIA and DOD began using drones extensively, especially in the Middle East, for both reconnaissance and direct strikes. Today, drones are everywhere and used for everything. Russia is using them in Ukraine and Georgia, ISIS used them in Syria and Iraq, the Taliban have used them in Afghanistan, and, of course, the United States uses them across the globe, including on U.S. soil (the FAA authorized the use of drones in 2006, namely the MQ-1 and MQ-9, to fly in U.S. airspace, ostensibly for Search & Rescue missions). Drones have also entered the commercial sector, with uses in recreation, entertainment, environmental monitoring and research.

Guerrillas, especially, have seen a great opportunity to use drones as force multipliers, and there are a great number of applications that guerrillas can use them for. Drones, while acting in several roles, really serve one purpose: to mitigate the threat of loss of life to human fighters. For guerrillas, every life is the strongest asset the force can have, so mitigating loss of life is extremely important. This is where drones come in.

Some of the applications that guerrillas can use drones for include:

- ISTAR
- Strikes
- SEAD/SED

ISTAR

ISTAR: Intelligence, Surveillance, Target Acquisition, and Reconnaissance.

Drones performing ISTAR are very powerful for guerrilla forces. From the air, new patterns can emerge, and new information can be presented. For guerrillas, having accurate and up-to-date information is critical, so using drones to perform ISTAR operations should be a prime focus for any guerrilla force. Drones operating in ISTAR roles can enable recon teams to collect intelligence remotely, enabling them to relay critical information faster and more safely to tactical decisionmakers in the field and leadership back at camp.

It is important to note that drones utilized by government and municipal entities are often outfitted with advanced technology, like FLIR and digitally enhanced cameras, which enable drones like the MQ-1 to detect heat signatures from up to 10,000 feet. Local and county police also often have equipment on aircraft that can zoom in on small items like license plates from several miles away. This level of capability simply cannot be replicated by guerrillas. However, with determination and ingenuity, guerrillas can use commercially available technology to *attempt* to increase the ISTAR capabilities of their drones and expand their intelligence gathering capabilities.

<u>STRIKE</u>

Drones as we know them have been conducting strike missions since the Vietnam war. They either carry munitions that can be fired remotely or they themselves are the munition. Strike missions are especially important for guerrillas, and, depending on the capability of the guerrilla, can help reduce collateral damage while also still hurting the enemy.

ISIS, Russia, and Ukraine have used commercially available drones to drop grenades, small mortar shells, and other munitions onto soft targets. In some cases, drones were designed to carry heavier ordnance, which was highly effective against armor and static emplacements like bunkers and mortar pits. Dropping explosives onto unsuspecting targets can have extremely powerful psychological effects on the enemy force.

Other groups developed fixed wing suicide drones, which are mounted with a live-feed camera, loaded with explosives and remotely guided into a target, detonating themselves during the impact. These drones are often very cheap to construct, or they can be made with found E-waste. Fixed wing drones can be mass produced, and can be used to target specific individuals, as well as to saturate an area and distract a force with multiple impacts.

<u>SEAD/SED</u>

SEAD/SED is Suppression of Enemy Air Defenses/Suppression of Enemy Defenses. Traditionally, SEAD is intended to destroy another force's anti-air capabilities.

For conventional groups, it is standard to establish a command center in a highly defendable location. This can be in a city, such as Kuala Lumpur during the Malayan Emergency, or another strategically important location like an airbase, such as Bagram airbase in Afghanistan. For our purposes, these locations will be known as *hardpoints*. These hardpoints are often impossible for guerrillas to attack in any effective way. Islamic terrorists have used suicide attacks against hardpoints, but the attack was almost always stopped at the checkpoint into the hardpoint and did nothing to dislodge the conventional forces.

This makes it difficult, if not impossible, for guerrilla forces to operate in certain areas. Something that guerrillas can do to weaken these locations is to use fixed wing drones for SEAD/SED. As discussed previously, drones are often used for strike missions, and can either release munitions onto a target or detonate themselves on the target. These hardpoints are defended by minefields, checkpoints, mobile and static security forces, static weapon emplacements, anti-air defenses, obstacles for personnel and vehicles, and, depending on what types of units are stationed within the hardpoint, armor or air support (which can also be available or on-station, even if not based out of the hardpoint itself). All these security elements form a net of security for the hardpoint, and so if a guerrilla force seeks to weaken, infiltrate or even overrun a hardpoint, then the first step is to rip a hole in the net. The guerrilla can then either slip through the tiny hole, or intentionally continue ripping. The more holes in the net, the less concentrated a defensive response might be. Using drones to saturate and overwhelm the defending forces, rip open holes in the "net" by striking fences, gates, or fortified positions, and to gather intelligence on these positions is critical.

Recent examples of this would be the Battles of Wanat and Kamdesh in Afghanistan (albeit, in neither battle did the Taliban field drones). In both cases, the Taliban identified the strongest security tools within the remote American positions and eliminated them at the very beginning of the battles (knocking out a TOW launcher and mortar pit at Wanat and a mortar pit at Kamdesh). Neither site was hardly comparable to major hardpoints like Bagram, but the principle applies. Similar to how the Finnish forces used Motti tactics against the Soviets in the Winter War, unconventional attacks on hardpoints may be conducted by creating small, manageable pockets of defenders and handling each pocket one-by-one, rather than engaging the entire site at once and inevitably running out of momentum or resources.

The Taliban attacked Wanat and Kamdesh by identifying the links within the security net of both sites and began cutting away at it. In both cases, the Taliban was able to briefly overrun the sites and inflict severe damage. It is worth mentioning that response times must be considered. In the case of Wanat, air support was overhead within 30 minutes of the attack. At Kamdesh, however, the air response took much longer, at which point U.S. and coalition soldiers had already lost much of COP Keating and had fallen back to a tight perimeter.

Had the Taliban had access to the drones that ISIS pioneered in Syria and Iraq, it is likely that the hardpoints in Afghanistan would have seen more attacks. Remote outposts such as COP Keating in Wanat especially would have been either abandoned or overrun very early in the war. By suppressing the defenses of these hardpoints, it becomes possible for fighters to move in and directly engage the defenders following initial SEAD/SED actions.

Of course, this concept of guerrilla-SEAD/SED is not a perfect solution. Most modern militaries possess weapons that can combat incoming aircraft, including drones. And as drones proliferate further and further each year, these same militaries are increasing their anti-drone arsenals to include shoulder-mounted jammers as well as ballistic and laser-based anti-drone capabilities. Enemy capabilities should be surveilled and mapped out long before a plan of action is made.

SIGNATURE MANAGEMENT

Since the beginning of the global war on terror, and especially during the administration of U.S. President Barrack Obama, there has been an unprecedented proliferation of unmanned aerial systems (UAS). Many UAS developed by the U.S. have been shared with NATO and EU allies and have seen extensive use in the Middle East, Africa, and Ukraine. Traditional adversaries to the West, including Iran, China, Russia, and North Korea, have developed their own UAS (mostly of original design, but sometimes copying western systems). These tools have been present in most 21st century conflicts and, because of their proliferation, should be expected to be present and active in all future conflicts. Even in peacetime drones are everywhere, and most western nations have some legal precedent allowing military or intelligence agencies to employ drones in domestic airspaces. Knowing this, any group involved in or anticipating conflict should alter current SOPs or develop new ones to mitigate enemy UAS capabilities.

UAS and their pilots must content with the task of patrolling and surveilling massive swaths of space. This task is simplified by two things: (1) Gathered intelligence that narrows down the area to be surveilled or patrolled and (2) Evidence of activity on the ground (i.e., shine from equipment or smoke from a fire). For the guerrilla, mitigating the power that UAS have in the battlespace begins and ends with camouflaging all gear and personnel and minimizing any signatures emitted.

In 2020, the United States Marine Corps released a publication intended to aid the infantry battalion in interrupting and weakening the ISTAR capabilities of enemy UAS. This publication, titled *SIGMAN: Camouflage SOP*, begins by detailing, broadly, the process in which a group can train and prepare to operate in a modern environment saturated with UAS.

1. **Disperse into small elements and displace often.** Dispersing prevents the group from being identified together and risking excessive casualties. Dispersing is a form of decentralization. It also prevents any distinguishable shapes from appearing, which can appear if the group bunches together.
2. **Find a concealed site and conform to terrain.** The site could be against the side of a mountain or hill, or in a valley or gorge. Tents and dwellings should be camouflaged with local vegetation. Using shadow and shape to hide from UAS is key as well. Trees, mountains, and hills will cast their shadows differently throughout the day. This should be considered.
3. **Operate at night and in difficult weather.** Detection at night can be difficult, even with heat detecting technology that is present on almost all military-grade UAS. Additionally, difficult weather such as high winds, low clouds, rain, snow, and fog can impair UAS operability, so it would be ideal to train and operate at these times whenever possible.
4. **Camouflage all people, positions, and equipment.** Camouflage is intended to break up colors, shapes, and patterns that are easily detected by the human eye. These patterns are especially detectable from the air. The dome of a tent or the outline of a vehicle are distinct, and do not occur naturally. Using local vegetation, camo netting, and strict discipline on light, noise, heat, trash and waste will help keep positions concealed.

5. **Minimize movement.** Any movement should be done at night or at times where UAS capabilities are weakened, like dusk, dawn, or during difficult weather. Any other time presents an often unnecessary risk of discovery.

6. **Post an air guard.** An air guard is an assigned individual, or team of individuals, whose purpose is to monitor the air for any sign of aircraft or UAS and alert friendlies.

7. **Plan to operate under UAS.** All planning and actions should be imagined through the lens of UAS. How a UAS might observe an event, or how a UAS might operate should be considerations when planning or operating. Additionally, it may be useful to operate under the premise that there is always a UAS in the sky. This can guarantee that the enemy's vote is considered.

8. **Inspect friendly positions from the enemy point of view.** Friendly forces should attempt to observe friendly positions from the air. This can help planners develop SOPs around movement, construction, and other actions that can prevent detection. Understanding yourself begins with understanding the enemy's perception of you. This can be done with commercially available quadcopter drones. Drones can be outfitted with thermal cameras as well.

All actions done in the field could result in being spotted by UAS, so precautions should be taken. Groups should train extensively under these conditions. Doing so will reduce strain and forced adaptation when a situation arises where UAS are being deployed against the group.

Assassination is an act of deliberate and selective killing. Historically, assassination has been a great tool for guerrilla forces, as it has the potential to reduce collateral damage while simultaneously eliminating high-level influential individuals or groups within military, social, or political circles.

Assassinations are generally meant to accomplish three things:

1. **To send a message.** This message can be one of warning, or of strength, or to terrify other high-level officials into hiding or rash action. The attempt alone can send the message.
2. **To eliminate a threat.** Some high-level individuals can be so influential or iconic that their very presence inspires an enemy force. Killing them can destroy morale and momentum.
3. **To demoralize.** The death of important individuals can hinder or even cripple a cause or force.

Eliminating individuals or groups can either destroy the morale of the enemy or embolden them. Thus, assassination should not be a hasty action for a guerrilla force. Potential ramifications should be contemplated at length, though not all will be seen immediately. With planning, assassinations can be done to intentionally replace an individual with another who may be more malleable or amenable. It should be remembered that guerrillas rarely win wars through force, and assassination can be used strategically in pursuit of a politically sound solution.

Assassinations can be accomplished in several ways. Firearms, explosives, and poisons are the most common methods in modern times. Governments have used nerve agents like Novichok and Sarin, or radioactive isotopes like Polonium-210. Terror groups have also used nerve agents like Sarin, but also ricin, which can be manufactured naturally. Drones can be used in targeted assassinations, limiting collateral damage that might be present in a traditional shooting or bombing. Successful assassinations stem from sound and timely intelligence gathering.

We have discussed, at length, the need for guerrillas to be resourceful. With the technological superiority that conventional forces have, ingenuity is not a talent that should be neglected. Conventional forces will seek to use their more powerful assets to control unconventional groups, such as heavy armor and mechanized infantry. Guerrillas in the 20th and 21st centuries found powerful ways to counter these assets.

IEDs

Improvised Explosive Devices (IEDs) are homemade explosives made from commonly available materials, such as storebought chemicals and scavenged pipes. Such devices saw, and continue to see, extensive use throughout the world for good reason. IEDs are among the primary reasons that the United States failed to accomplish its objectives in Iraq and Afghanistan, resulting in tens of thousands of American deaths and casualties as well as the catastrophic U.S. withdrawals.

Generally speaking, there are five distinct parts to an IED:

1. **The Switch.** The switch is the device used to "set off" the IED. Some examples of a switch include pressure plates, cell phones, and infrared lasers.
2. **The Main Charge.** The main charge is the explosive itself. Some groups, such as ISIS, created their own proprietary explosives. Others, like the IRA, obtained pre-made explosives like Semtex and C4.
3. **The Container.** The container is what holds the explosive and other components.
4. **The Detonator.** The detonator is a smaller explosive, electrical charge, or impact that detonates the main charge.
5. **The Power Supply.** The power supply powers the switch and/or the detonator.

With these components (often scavenged or store-bought), insurgents, guerrillas, and extremist groups have developed IEDs to employ against their political and military opponents, sometimes to great success. However, conventional forces have not allowed IEDs to proliferate without contest. Defense contractors have begun to develop tools that can identify IEDs from stand-off distances. Such tools can identify electrical components or radio signals that may be emitted from any devices. These can still be countered. Additionally, convoys and patrols have begun carrying vehicle mounted and man-portable jamming equipment that can completely counter remotely controlled explosives. The answer to these has been any analog-triggering devices, such as pressure plates or electrical cable.

An EFP (Explosively Formed Penetrator) is a self-forming warhead that can pierce armor and damage, disable, or destroy many up-armored vehicles. These have seen use across the globe during the GWOT. Specifically, Iran's Quds Force has both provided the devices and the knowledge to produce them to Shia extremists in Syria and Iraq. In Iraq, EFPs make up more than half of the IEDs that have been used to attack U.S. and Coalition convoys. The EFP container is usually cylindrical, like a barrel or tube. The cylindrical container will be topped with a concave metal lid. This lid, when the EFP detonates, will propel forward at a high velocity and crumble into projectile.

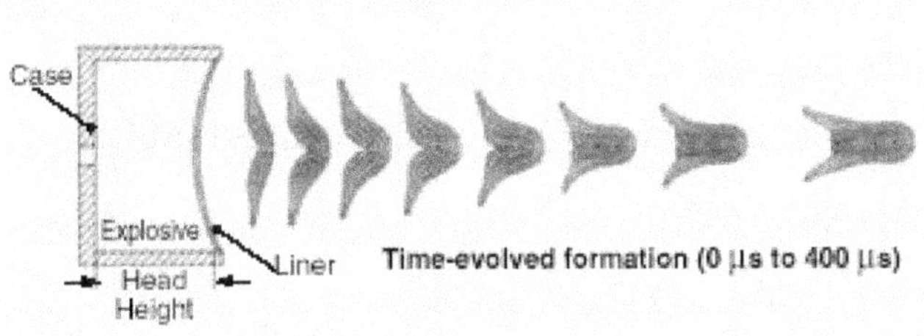

(EFP formation process from detonation)

The strength of the EFP lies in its ability to penetrate armor, and it is used historically to ambush armored convoys. EFPs can be small (as small as a toaster or basketball) and can be concealed on roads or along walls, so that the projectile enters the armored vehicle from the side rather than from beneath. Larger EFPs can be buried or concealed with trash along roadways or even suspended from above. EFPs are mostly ineffective against foot patrols and are reserved for use against armored vehicles and convoys.

Directional Frag Charges (DFCs) work similarly to claymores, in that they are detonated by a explosive charge intended to propel small pieces of material (usually metal, like shavings, nuts, bolts, screws, washers, or BB pellets) in a particular direction. DFCs can be extremely dangerous for forces without armor support, or in unarmored vehicles. DFCs are especially useful in ambushes and defensive operations. Low-yield DFCs can be used to injure, rather than kill, putting a strain on pre-hospital healthcare providers and systems, reducing combat effectiveness or operational tempo. DFCs are not accurate from long distances. DFCs are normally used near the target.

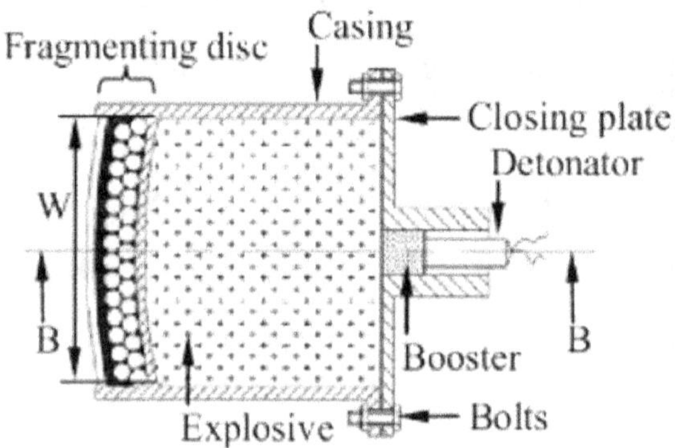

(Example of a DFC with metal pellets for frag)

What is now known as Post Traumatic Stress Disorder (PTSD) has existed for as long as humans have engaged in conflict. Neanderthals, Mongols, Romans, and the American warfighter have all experienced it. It has gone by many names including shell shock and combat fatigue. In the American Civil War, veterans often experienced unexplainable cardiac issues, like heart disease and arrhythmias. This was simply called "Soldier's Heart" or "irritable heart" and little was done in the way of real research, diagnosis, prevention, or treatment. Historically, the prevailing idea was that PTSD was the fault of the soldier. That it was an inherent weakness within that led to the condition. It was not until the Vietnam war, however, that PTSD was first coined as a term and researchers began putting time and money into studying the condition. At this time, the longstanding idea of the "weak minded soldier" was challenged. The American Psychiatric Association (APA) concluded in 1980 that the cause of PTSD lied with the trauma experienced by the soldier, not by any internal weakness.

The sudden interest was not uncalled for. The Vietnam War was especially violent, and such violence often came on suddenly and in extreme degrees. Use of IEDs, ambushes, and artillery attacks left soldiers with serious psychological and physiological conditions that they returned home with. Following the war, research into PTSD slowed. When the Global War on Terrorism began, however, the interest was renewed with vigor.

Of 60,000 screened OEF/OIF veterans, nearly 14% were diagnosed with PTSD, most of them being active duty and deployed to combat zones. Realistically though, the number is higher. A 2020 survey concluded that 83% of all veterans since 9/11 have experienced or will experience PTSD.

With these numbers in mind, let us look at estimated PTSD rates from previous conflicts. It is estimated that 15-30% of Vietnam veterans experience PTSD at some point. Based on hospitalization and service records, it is estimated that 3-37% of World War II veterans experience PTSD at some point. Even with a respectable margin of error and respecting the fact that diagnoses and treatment were largely nonexistent in these conflicts, the difference in PTSD rates from these conflicts to the GWOT is tremendous.

Based on these numbers, we must ask ourselves what was so different about the GWOT that caused healthcare providers and researchers to take a historically unprecedented look at a psychological condition like PTSD. Based on current diagnostic standards, one of the main criteria for diagnosing acute and chronic PTSD require that a person experiences events that threatened death or serious harm to themselves or others. This, of course, will be very common in warzones. However, the difference we are seeing in PTSD rates from previous conflicts to the GWOT may not be related to the *actual* threat of death or harm (which has been faced in all prior conflicts), but the uncertainty of the threat of death or harm.

The suddenness of an IED attack would surely present the threat of death or harm to oneself or others. Route Irish in Iraq, for example, was a Main Supply Route (MSD) running from Baghdad International Airport to the Coalition-held Green Zone. Route Irish became colloquially known as "IED Alley" due to the number of insurgent IEDs detonated against patrols and convoys. The threat weighed on the minds of all coalition troops. At any moment, they could step on or drive past an IED that could detonate. Or they could not, but they would run the risk every time they crossed the wire. A convoy could drive the same route for a year, but all it takes is one IED attack to spark uncertainty. This uncertainty, combined with the *actual* threat of death or harm from an IED create a unique distress that is unseen in previous conflicts. The proliferation of the IED throughout the Middle East is directly responsible for higher rates of PTSD in American and Coalition servicemembers.

Simply knowing the symptoms of acute and chronic PTSD could cause distress in soldiers patrolling areas known to harbor IEDs. Guerrilla groups could use this to their advantage in propaganda or psychological warfare campaigns. Symptoms of PTSD include recurring memories of the traumatic event, emotional distress, avoiding situations or areas that present similar threats, hopelessness, irritability and violent outbursts, memory loss, and constant heightened alertness. These symptoms could make functioning in normal life extremely difficult, so the heightened stress of combat and the perceived risk of IEDs or sudden attacks would amplify these symptoms, reducing combat effectiveness and, over time, willingness to wage a counterinsurgency.

Conventional forces, especially Western navies, own the waterways of the planet. It is unrealistic to expect anything otherwise. However, naval powers are not untouchable, nor are they able to monitor or control every ship or waterway. Unconventional forces can use this to their advantage. While unconventional forces are unable to directly contest the modern fleets of carriers, cruisers, cutters, and destroyers, they can harass these vessels and maneuver around them to accomplish their tactical and strategic objectives.

In 2008, for example, the Pakistan-based Islamist terror group Lashkar-e-Taiba infiltrated the Indian city of Mumbai from the Arabian Sea. Prior to the attack, the fighters infiltrated Mumbai posing as students and reconnoitered the sites they intended to attack. The gunmen left the coastal Pakistani city of Karachi by stowing away on a cargo ship bound for India. Eventually, the gunmen disembarked the ship and hijacked an indigenous fishing trawler and used that to get closer to Mumbai. The Indian Coast Guard did contact them at one point, but the gunmen raised a white flag and pretended to be lost, killing both Indian Coast Guard officers and continuing to their target. Finally, several inflatable rubber boats operated by Lashkar-e-Taiba operatives deployed from Mumbai to pick up the gunmen from the trawler and bring them ashore.

The leadership and members of Lashkar-e-Taiba knew that infiltrating India from known land routes or border crossings would create an unnecessary risk of discovery and using any non-commercial boat transports obtained in Pakistan would potentially lead to scrupulous inspection by the Navy or Coast Guard. Keeping in mind the SOPs of the Indian forces and the maritime trade routes in the Arabian Sea, they were able to infiltrate Mumbai from the sea which was completely unexpected. Similar courses of action could be taken both to infiltrate an area or to escape.

Additionally, rivers around the world have acted as smuggling routes for goods and supplies for criminal enterprises and guerrilla forces alike. In Africa and Southeast Asia, river pirates still raid oil tankers, cargo ships, and barges to steal food, raw materials to be sold on the black market, and military equipment. Some rivers in Europe still see criminal activity, such as on the Danube. In most cases, criminals will board moored ships at night using small inflatable boats, jon boats, kayaks, canoes, or sampans. In North America, the Rio Grande River is used to smuggle arms, drugs, and people between the U.S. and Mexico. Though the Rio Grande, unlike many rivers in Asia, Africa, and parts of Europe, is heavily monitored with watercraft, aircraft, and shoreside patrols. Still, Mexican cartels use the route with a considerable degree of success. Guerrillas could use similar smuggling routes in pursuit of their goals or sustainment.

TEAM BUILDING

For guerrillas, it can be difficult to create an atmosphere of trust and dedication. Conventional force HUMINT teams and state intelligence apparatuses regularly seek to infiltrate teams and undermine trust within teams, communities, and organizations. The most effective way to combat these operations begins, of course, with counterintelligence efforts. But infiltration efforts can be undermined by developing strong bonds between teams within the organization.

Generally speaking, teams can be built three ways:

1. Customs & Traditions
2. Competition
3. Shared Suffering

Customs & Traditions

Customs and traditions make up the identity of an organization. Through customs and traditions, an organization can create a shared identity that each member can identify with and find purpose within. Many modern military units have a motto (often in Latin) that echo that unit's history or values. The motto should reflect something real and tangible, such as a shared history or value. An example would be the U.S. Marine Corps 2nd Battalion, 5th Marines motto of "Retreat Hell!" which dates to their service in France during WWI. Similarly, the Vermont National Guard's motto, "Put the Vermonters ahead," dates to their action at the Battle of

Gettysburg in the American Civil War. The Green Berets motto "De Oppresso Liber" reflects their specialized mission in unconventional warfare, which often has them arming, training, and fighting with indigenous guerrilla forces. This shared identity comes with time and experience working together and developing the unit.

Groups can further create a communal identity through customs like rituals, indoctrination, training, music, or tactics.

Groups can take advantage of competition to help build trust and camaraderie. Through competition, team members can challenge themselves and others to be better. Some examples of competitions that can build teams include:

- Team-based marksmanship competitions
- Obstacle courses that require teamwork
- Productive combatives (pugil sticks, martial arts, etc.)
- Athletic competitions

Through competition, teams can develop individual and group attributes like grit, determination, and resilience. Teams can also learn to rely on each other when it is needed, and not when it is convenient. Cooperation is critical to teams and learning how each team member thinks and moves in moments of pressure and stress is critical to developing a functional, trusting team.

Suffering is bound to happen in any organization, especially one that is organized to participate in conflict. Suffering should never be a thing that any one person carries, but something that is shared amongst all members, especially leadership. Suffering should not be first experienced in a time of high risk, such as combat. Instead, organizations should seek to incorporate discomfort and stress into some of their trainings. This shared suffering will help bring members of the group closer together as they find solutions to the problems they face or fail in the process.

The shared suffering experienced by individuals within the group will help build bonds that will be harder to break or sever, especially by outside forces. Creating these bonds is critical to developing a unified, cohesive team. Suffering should not be done just for the sake of it. It should have a purpose that each team member can understand, such as a difficult backcountry hiking trip or a Field Training Exercise (FTX) after a training series. gWhen individuals cannot find purpose in their suffering, whether it is alone or shared, they begin to look for ways out or coping methods. These are generally going to be destructive or erosive to the group, so leaders should make sure that team members understand their purpose within the team or mission.

The guerrilla has many challenges he must face to find success on the modern battlefield. He cannot call air support. He does not have extensive medical or rehabilitation systems. He does not have satellites that orbit the planet, feeding him a steady stream of intelligence on troop and supply movements. He does not have tanks, or artillery, or destroyers, or carriers, or bombers.

The guerrilla wins from his willpower, his ability to fight for years on end, decades even, without losing sight of the better world he fights for. The guerrilla earns his place by outlasting his opponent who has every technological asset at their disposal. He earns his place by outthinking his opponent, by not relying on any asset but his mind, by being cunning, barbaric, and decisive. He earns the love of his fellow man by being compassionate, selfless, and brave.

The only assets that the guerrilla can ever truly count on are his mind and his body. Through education, experience, and constant training, the guerrilla can hone these assets while his conventional opponents become reliant on technology and administrative processes. The diligent guerrilla will identify the weaknesses of his enemy and exploit them at every juncture. He should be constantly setting the standard and defining the battlespace, being proactive and ever ready to alter his procedures to take advantage of opportunities that he creates. Being reactive to the enemy only guarantees death and failure.

Chapter 10:

COUNTERINSURGENCY

"Thus, counterinsurgency is at heart an adaptation battle: a struggle to rapidly develop and learn new techniques and apply them in a fast-moving, high-threat environment, bringing them to bear before the enemy can evolve in response, and rapidly changing them as the environment shifts."

-   David Kilcullen

One way that guerrillas succeed is by understanding their enemies as well as they understand themselves. The first and primary enemy to any unconventional group is going to be the counterinsurgency. Like guerrillas, counterinsurgents seek to gain public support and wear their opponent down through time and attrition. Unlike the guerrilla, however, the counterinsurgent can seize and hold defined territory. However, counterinsurgents are often plagued by general inefficiency, operational red tape, internal political disputes, and cowardice or incompetence (often both) in the highest levels of military and political leadership.

Additionally, counterinsurgencies may fall into the trap of not having unified, well-understood strategy at all. Instead, they may focus simply on attrition, or going from firefight to firefight. This was common in Afghanistan, since the Taliban was often able to engage from a distance and then withdraw from the area before U.S. forces could orchestrate a cohesive response. Guerrillas can use these known pitfalls, combined with an understanding of previously successful counterinsurgent strategies, to combat, undermine, and ultimately defeat a more powerful, well organized, and centralized foe.

Each counterinsurgency (CI) is unique. The approaches are unique and are based on factors like key terrain and social or political considerations, however the one unifying piece is that the counterinsurgent seeks to separate the insurgent from the civilian. By doing so, the counterinsurgent can more effectively engage the insurgent while seizing space and solidifying its influence over the civilian population. The guerrilla should avoid this at all costs, either by operating clandestinely within the same area (often a city) or by seizing and holding his own territory (often in rural or peri-urban areas). Having an ironclad relationship with the local population also weakens the counterinsurgent's' ability to divide the civilian and the guerrilla.

Clear-Hold-Build

The Clear-Hold-Build strategy requires that an area be cleared of insurgent activity. Once the area is clear, counterinsurgents begin to solidify their control over the area by creating hardpoints, establishing control or influence over social or political institutions, and saturating the area with CI security forces. Finally, the counterinsurgency begins to pursue social, political, and economic development projects that are intended to shape the space to fit the needs and wants of the counterinsurgency. These projects are aimed to provide the locals with improvements to education and healthcare access, physical and political security, or otherwise some improvement to quality of life.

The Clear-Hold-Built strategy has been used since the British implemented it during the Malayan Emergency. British appointees Harold Briggs and Gerald Templer each contributed to the successful efforts to physically separate the communist Malayan National Liberation Army (MNLA) insurgents from the civilian population. The MNLA operated mostly out of the jungles and swamps of the Malay Peninsula, where they enjoyed freedom of movement, an abundance of food, and plentiful support from locals. The British removed rural civilians from the presence of the MNLA by way of the Briggs Plan, a forced resettlement of over 500,000 civilians into concentration camps known as "New Villages." Once the civilians were physically separated from the insurgents, the British counterinsurgency began focusing on eliminating the MNLA food sources and wearing them down through attrition. British forces, as discussed earlier, would use former-MNLA guides and trackers to lead ambush parties into the swamps and jungles. Each insurgent killed was a morale boost for the counterinsurgency.

With the success seen by the British counterinsurgency in Malaya, clear-hold-built became a critical piece, if not the standard, for counterinsurgency strategy. However, it has not seen the same degree of success since its implementation in Malaya. The United States placed a focus on the clear-hold-build strategy in Iraq and Afghanistan.

Iraq: Clear

The U.S.-led coalition was able to invade and conquer Iraq in less than a month. Early on, Iraqi forces decided to fight both a conventional and unconventional war. Caches were created across the country in anticipation for an insurgency. This preparation made it difficult for the U.S. to fully clear any city, even Baghdad.

Iraq: Hold

Because the insurgency began in earnest, coalition forces struggled to hold much territory early on. Iraq is unique in that much of the insurgency occurred within urban areas, which was not the case in previous implementations of clear-hold-build. Because of this, U.S. forces did not truly hold any significant territory throughout the country. Instead, the only territory held by coalition forces was the Green Zone (the political and military administrative hub in Baghdad), and several bases, camps, and combat outposts. From these sites, coalition forces began targeting the insurgency. Following The Surge in 2007, instances of violence and the number of fatalities throughout Iraq did decrease for a time, but eventually increased once again. Major cities, like Baghdad, Najaf, Fallujah, and Samara were never truly held or pacified, and the U.S. eventually handed over all gained territory to Iraqi government authorities.

Iraq: Build

Shortly following the invasion, the United States Congress authorized nearly $21 Billion in funding through the Iraq Relief & Reconstruction Fund (IRRF). The intent of the IRRF is to fund infrastructure repair and development initiatives throughout Iraq. Through the fund, improvements have been made to water treatment and sewage plants, electricity generation systems, telecommunications networks, and agriculture programs. Schools and hospitals were also repaired, equipped, funded, or built through the IRRF and other funds. Additionally, the fund allocated $5.1B of the $21B for security programs. This $5.1B has been used to arm and train both the Iraqi army as well as the Iraqi police.

While the U.S. and its coalition partners were able to defeat the Iraqi insurgency militarily, it did not win the war and the clear-hold-build strategy did not deliver the intended results, nor did the U.S. achieve its strategic objectives in Iraq. Extremism in Iraq was not exterminated, nor was a modern democracy installed. In fact, the opposite is true. When the U.S. withdrew from Iraq in 2011, it left a power vacuum that allowed ISIS to rapidly gain power, directly oppose the Iraqi army, and gain vast amounts of territory throughout Iraq and Syria. The reign of the Islamic State was extremely detrimental to Iraq, and only introduced more death, destruction, and extremism.

Afghanistan: Clear

Like Iraq, the Taliban regime in Afghanistan fell rather quickly. With the combination of an air campaign and U.S. Special Forces working in conjunction with the Northern Alliance and Pashtun militias. Just 37 days after the first U.S. airstrikes, Kabul falls to coalition and Northern Alliance forces, and Hamid Karzai is installed by the U.S. and UN.

Afghanistan: Hold

For several years, the U.S. held ground against the Taliban. However, in July of 2006, the Taliban resurfaces with heavy fighting throughout the south, mixed with large numbers of suicide attacks. This occurred due to the ineffectiveness of the elected Afghan government, U.S., and coalition peacekeeping failures, and advancements in training and recruitment for the Taliban gained in Pakistan. The U.S. never fully held the south of the country, including the three key provinces of Helmand, Kandahar, and Nimruz (all of which shared a border with Pakistan). The U.S. did enjoy control over many of the urban centers in Afghanistan. But given the fact that the country is very rural and rugged, coalition forces placed very little emphasis on the rural villages and settlements from which the Taliban gained most of its supplies, support, and refuge. There was an attempt to expand U.S. influence into rural areas through the Village Stability Operations (VSO) program, which was essentially a local defense program intended to train, arm, and educate rural areas against the Taliban and its influence. The program failed, however, when political expediency took root and military commanders focused more on quantity (simply increasing the number of VSO sites without guaranteeing success) versus quality (sacrificing the effectiveness and reliability of established sites). Because of this, the U.S. was never able to truly hold territory outside of major urban centers or established bases like Bagram Air Base.

Afghanistan: Build

Afghanistan was also granted a large sum dedicated to reconstruction and development of key infrastructure. Congress appropriated more than $38 Billion to fund these projects. Expansions of democratic institutions were key as the U.S. wanted to create a modern democracy based on of Kabul, but other programs included the development of telecom services, water and sewage access, education initiatives, healthcare drives, school and hospital construction plans, and funding for VSO sites and Provisional Reconstruction Teams.

Historically, the clear-hold-build strategy seems to only work in urbanized areas. It worked in Malaya because the British were able to mobilize hundreds of thousands of civilians into intentionally constructed towns that were guarded and monitored for insurgent activity. The system also worked in Iraq for a time and may have been a success if the U.S. had spent more time in-country and removed much of the political red tape.

Clear-hold-build did not work in Afghanistan, however, due to the rural nature of the country. Many of the towns and villages were majority conservative Pashtun, and directly identified with the Taliban. While the U.S. consistently held territory in more progressive city centers like Kabul, Mazar-i-Sharif, and Jalalabad, it was difficult for U.S. forces to establish any meaningful, long-lasting presence in the rural areas where the Taliban thrived. Therefore, the cord between the Taliban and their support base was never severed.

Clear-hold-build has been the foundational counterinsurgency strategy for most western powers because holding territory is what conventional forces understand. However, the guerrilla does not need to hold territory. The guerrilla needs to be able to flow through territory while having access to their support base. Clear-hold-build has its uses and has been used to great effect against insurgent forces, but it is not always the solution.

In a counterinsurgency, state intelligence organizations work closely with special operations forces to complete specialized, often surgical missions. These missions are done at the tactical and strategic levels, and are conducted independently or with conventional support, such as infantry. Throughout the history of modern counterinsurgencies, special forces have played a key part by:

- Engaging with locals through KLEs or other Civil Affairs actions/programs
- Gathering or generating intelligence for future SOF or conventional operations
- Supporting conventional missions
- Protecting key individuals (diplomatic staff, political or military leaders, etc.)
- Direct action against insurgents (raids, ambushes, etc.)

All missions that SOF engage in require intelligence to be executed successfully. When Afghanistan became a top U.S. priority following 9/11, the CIA formed the Center for Counterterrorism (CTC) and began working closely with SOF deployed to Northern Afghanistan. Throughout the duration of the war in Afghanistan, the CIA, the Defense Intelligence Agency (DIA), and other intelligence services worked closely with the various SOF units that the U.S. and coalition forces deployed. Oftentimes, these intelligence services were responsible for funneling arms and funding to local militias opposing the Taliban and Al-Qaeda, as well as providing intelligence on militant targets in Afghanistan. Additionally, these agencies worked to manipulate the internal politics of Afghanistan and neighboring Pakistan to further reduce Taliban influence.

While the strategic objectives for the U.S. in Afghanistan were not met, integrating intelligence assets with SOF units yielded great results in terms of attrition. SOF units working with intelligence services were especially efficient in urban areas. The number of targets identified by intelligence assets led to an extremely high operational tempo at several points throughout the war.

Intelligence services have pursued similar activities across the globe, but particularly throughout the Middle East. Western and local services in Syria, Iraq, Jordan, Israel, and elsewhere have put a high premium on SOF-intelligence integration to combat insurgencies and extremism.

Arguably the most high-profile SOF missions in the global war on terror were Operation Neptune Spear and Operation Kayla Mueller.

Neptune Spear was the operation culminating in the decade-long hunt for Osama Bin Laden. The operation was the result of years of intelligence collection by the CIA. Bin Laden moved frequently between 2001 and 2011, and was only found at his safehouse in Abbottabad, Pakistan because of the CIAs ability to track Bin Laden's personal courier, Ibrahim Saeed Ahmed.

Operation Kayla Mueller, similarly, was the result of years of intelligence work done by the CIA and other services. The operation led to the death of Abu Bakr al-Baghdadi, leader and caliph of the Islamic State. The CIA was able to ascertain the location of al-Baghdadi's compound through a variety of means. Iraqi and Turkish intelligence agencies were able to capture and interrogate several high-ranking ISIS officials who gave details about al-Baghdadi's activities in Syria. Additionally, the Kurdish SDF (Syrian Defense Force) worked to gather intelligence on ISIS activities in Northwest Syria and handled a deep-cover informant within al-Baghdadi's security circle. A combination of these intelligence sources led the CIA to discover the location of al-Baghdadi's compound.

We can see based on these two operations that, while SOF units are incredibly capable warfighters, they are virtually useless in a strategic capacity without access to accurate and timely intelligence. There would be no raids on the Bin Laden and al-Baghdadi compounds were it not for the intelligence gathering efforts of countless individuals. The success of SOF units in their individual missions relies on a healthy operational relationship with intelligence services.

Previous periods in history required that the insurgent have physical access to the civilian population to disseminate propaganda. To a certain degree, that is still true today. However, the internet changed the landscape for insurgencies and counterinsurgencies. In the modern day, militants and propagandists can disseminate their message to millions via the internet, the dark web, and social media. In response, counterinsurgencies have been forced to expand their operations to include countering propaganda and Information Operations (IO).

IOs, broadly, are any operations that seek to influence, disrupt, or impede groups, public thought, or ongoing military/security operations. Some IOs focus specifically on manipulating public opinion or other civil factors, while others focus on specifically disrupting or misleading military actors. IOs can be conducted by all actors in a battlespace, including conventional forces, SOF, insurgents, and other paramilitary groups. IOs can be offensive or defensive in nature.

Offensive IOs are intended to attack the legitimacy of or trust in a force or institution, but also to influence or mislead enemy combatants through psychological operations. An example of an offensive IO would be Iraqi insurgents releasing video reels of IED detonations against U.S. coalition convoys, or the PIRA South Armagh Brigade's "sniper at work" signs.

Defensive IOs are intended to improve the capabilities of friendly forces, while reducing the effectiveness, operational tempo, or confidence of an enemy force. An example of a defensive IO would be a guerrilla group inflating its capabilities through psychological operations to alter the decision making of counterinsurgent leaders.

Information Operations are key to successful guerrilla movements. Accordingly, counterinsurgents place a heavy focus on countering guerrilla IOs. Counterinsurgencies have access to state media sources, so their messaging can come from more recognized or "official" sources. Additionally, their reach may be more extensive. Guerrillas may take advantage of these media outlets to disseminate their own propaganda. The first step in countering IOs is to conduct a SCAME analysis.

A SCAME analysis seeks to collate and analyze the content within the piece of messaging. SCAME is an acronym that stands for:

Source – what group/author published the messaging?

Content – what is the intent/objective/argument of the messaging?

Audience – who is the message for? what is the intended group's reaction?

Media – what medium was used to disseminate the messaging?

Effects – what effect is the messaging having on the audience/observers?

Each aspect of the SCAME analysis needs to be explored from a detached perspective to effectively understand the IO, which then enables friendly forces to counter the IO through their own messaging.

For a counterinsurgency to progress, it must be able to maintain all the operational success it may have had. Consolidating gains begins after military dominance has been established. In some cases, consolidating gains can look like creating a string of hard military targets (camps, forts, etc.) along transport routes to prevent insurgent fighters from physically returning to the area. Such programs are known as the *"Hedgehog defense,"* conceptualized by French officers during the First Indochina War. Additionally, consolidating gains could look like establishing inroads with the local population, successful decapitation operations, or standing up a stable civil governing authority. If the counterinsurgency forces are unable to maintain and build off their successes, then the guerrilla forces will return with a renewed approach.

Any counterinsurgency operation occurs in phases. This is known as a *notional phasing model.*

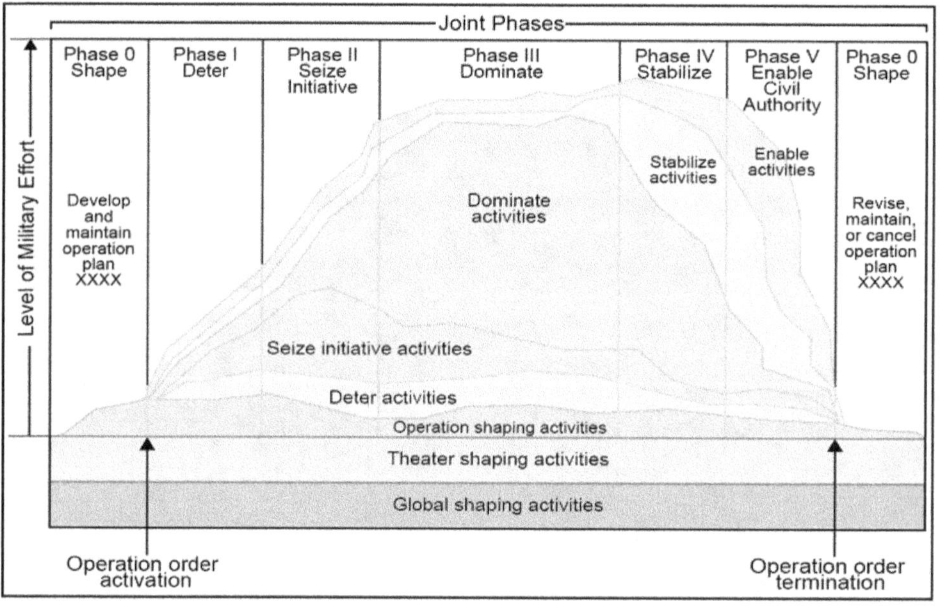

(Example of a Notional Phasing Model)

The phases may overlap or occur in nonsequential order, but consolidating gains traditionally occurs in Phases IV (Stabilization activities) and V (Enable Civil Authority activities).

During Phase IV, the focus shifts from active military operations to security operations. This is to reduce the impact of conflict on everyday life in a society. Returning society to a state of stability, or at least low intensity conflict, is a primary goal for any counterinsurgency. The U.S. attempted this phase after the invasion of Afghanistan and the toppling of the Taliban government. However, the rural nature of the country made stabilization difficult, as the militant forces would simply return to an area after U.S. coalition forces had left. The counterinsurgency may attempt to stand up a civilian led police or security force to oppose any remaining insurgent threats, while still utilizing special forces and intelligence assets to hunt down remaining fighters or leadership. Guerrillas may actively oppose counterinsurgent efforts in Phase IV by delegitimizing the civil leadership, while capitalizing on mismanagement and corruption within civil bodies.

During Phase V, supporting the civil government becomes the primary concern. This traditionally looks like enabling elections or installing ministers or presidents. The goal for the counterinsurgency is to create a stable civilian led government that conforms to the political and social ideals and standards of the political leadership behind the counterinsurgency. At this point, counterinsurgent military activity reaches its lowest point. This is usually when counterinsurgent forces withdraw from the area, region, or country and turn over security operations to the installed civil government.

If the counterinsurgency is unable to consolidate the gains it makes, then it is impossible for it to achieve its strategic objectives. The guerrilla may simply seek to prevent the counterinsurgency from gaining ground, either physically through territory gain, or through gaining support from the civilian population. By preventing the counterinsurgency from completing its strategic objectives, the guerrilla may be able to win simply by outlasting the counterinsurgency. Such an approach will take time and many lives, but at a certain point the counterinsurgent's will to fight will wane, or it will be eclipsed by the desire of the counterinsurgency's home country to withdraw from conflict.

Chapter 11:

LEADERSHIP

"He who cannot be a good follower, cannot be a good leader."

- **Aristotle**

Leadership, in many societies, is taught at a very early age. In western societies, which tend to lean towards individualism, many children are told to rebuke followership, and to always step up to lead. They are told that they should take charge and always stand up for their opinions in the face of criticism or conflict, and to never forsake their values. These are admirable teachings and are good foundations for critical thinking and self-respect. Somewhere along the way, however, there was a disconnect. Today, for many adults, to stand up for an opinion is to refuse to concede ground. Ingrained in the minds of many is that they are inherently right in all things, that their opinions are correct, their knowledge perfect, their morals just, and their actions without fault. This is dangerous, especially for times of conflict.

The reality is that not everyone is immediately capable of leading armies, groups, teams, or even themselves. Leaders are made, not born. Through education, discipline, and experience the leader is developed from a follower who executes the mission into someone who can see and guide others towards the "bigger picture" within an organization. Leaders, however, are not the linchpin of an organization as many believe. In fact, the leader and the follower serve unique purposes but are equally important in achieving the strategic goals of the organization. In this chapter, we will discuss what those purposes are, and how individuals can achieve their greatest potentials within their roles.

A common issue that any organization can face is excessive centralization. High level leaders, committees, or boards that make every minor decision for teams who are on the ground can lead to tunnel vision for the organization. Additionally, when the organization is centralized, it can be difficult to respond to rapidly changing conditions or developments in the field. Leaders who do not fully understand the situation on the ground, or who let their biases or predispositions guide them, simply cannot make the best judgement call on tactical operations. Attempts by leaders to excessively control decision making at the lowest levels have caused disaster in tactical situations and failures at the strategic level.

It is important, however, that unconventional groups do not balk at centralized leadership altogether. The solution to this conundrum could lie in Centralized Control-Decentralized Execution (CC-DE). This system enables leaders to guide tactical operations toward accomplishing strategic objectives, while enabling and trusting low-level decisionmakers to use their expertise and situational knowledge to operate with a large degree of autonomy. CC-DE avoids the pitfalls of extreme decentralization that many unconventional groups have fallen into. Helmuth Von Moltke, a Prussian field officer, is believed to be the first leader to incorporate CC-DE into military institutional decision making. This system was known as *Auftragstaktik*, or "mission tactics," and was used with great success by the Prussian Army and, subsequently, the German Wehrmacht invasions of Poland, Czechoslovakia, and France. Auftragstaktik was executed under the premise of extensive strategic planning and coordination of units or groups, combined with initiative-driven field leaders focused on tactical maneuvers.

Under CC-DE, strategic leaders should guarantee that their field leaders fully understand the leader's intent, as well as the strategic goal(s) of the organization, so that field leaders can effectively take tactical initiative in pursuit of the strategic objectives. Misunderstanding the strategic goals of the organization, or frequent changes to strategic objectives, can cause friction between leaders at the strategic and field levels, as well as operational failures at every level.

Excessive decentralization can lead to multiple groups existing independent of each other, targeting the same opponent, but pursuing different strategic objectives. History shows us that successful unconventional groups are decentralized in nature but have a cohesive strategy that they work towards, loosely following CC-DE doctrine. As the unconventional group gains success, power (political and military) and territory, the group has the potential to develop an official, public leadership structure that can begin to develop a more centralized institution (ideally using Mao's 3-Phase model).

For unconventional groups, it can be very dangerous to rely on a centralized leadership source because conventional forces often begin combat operations by pursuing decapitation strikes. If the group is too centralized, then a successful decapitation of its leadership could create chaos and disarray throughout the group. This has led to the failure and dissolution of countless insurgent groups, many of which have been forgotten to history.

LEADING FROM THE FRONT

All leaders should avoid insulating themselves from the discomfort or conflict that their team members and subordinates experience. For centuries, military leaders from Europe to Asia to North America and back enjoyed luxurious living conditions, ample food, clean water, and other amenities that their subordinates were forced to do without. These conditions that were afforded to leaders often created a distorted sense of reality for them, while creating resentment between the leader and his subordinates. These leaders were unable to effectively appreciate their subordinates, understand their opponent, or grasp the rapidly evolving conflict that they found themselves in.

Instead, a good leader is found living, working, fighting, and training with his men. This way he fully understands his own circumstances and limitations, as well as the capabilities of his opponent, and the dispositions of his men.

Chapter 12:

CONCLUSION

Guerrilla forces will forever be outmatched and outgunned, however, through training, planning, and dedication, the guerrilla may prevail. Ultimately, the guerrilla must be a learned man. At all times, the guerrilla should look to examples throughout history to see how conventional forces were defeated, how guerrillas were crushed, how free states were built, and how people could be liberated.

If the guerrilla refuses to learn, adapt, and set aside his ego, then he is doomed. He should always remind himself to place the safety and the freedom of his neighbor above everything, so that he may call on their support when needs. The guerrilla should be prepared to call on experts in their respective fields, so that they may be able to employ modern tools against his foes.

He should be ready and willing to lay down his life for the cause, and always call on his comrades to improve themselves physically, mentally, intellectually, and spiritually. The guerrilla should always fight for liberty, peace, and justice. Any other pursuit is folly, and the guerrilla will not be remembered by history as a freedom fighter, but as a terrorist. He should be guided by wisdom and tempered by morals.

It is the author's hope that the words in this volume will guide such

men in future conflicts, so that they may live, that they may protect

the lives of others, and that they may build societies that can

withstand tyranny, evil, and corruption.